# Alpha Man

## vs.

# GOD

### The Final Encounter in Men's Struggle for Significance

David O. Smith

12  11  10  9  8  7  6  5  4  3  2  1

GOD HAS A GREAT
PLAN FOR YOU!

JER 28:11

# Contents

# Introduction

## One Man's Story

Men want to be remembered. We long to make an impact, a legacy that outlives us. Success is admirable but significance defines us. As a newly-minted Harvard MBA, significance meant getting my mug on the cover of *Fortune Magazine*. How I got there was immaterial. I was prepared to outsmart and out-hustle the competition.

I was a typical alpha man: aggressive, driven, and achievement-oriented. Alphas envision bold changes for the world and possess the tenacity to make our dreams a reality. We are risk takers with great confidence in our instincts and resourcefulness. Winning is paramount; failure is not an option.

I landed a post in the fastest-growing division at New York's top marketing firm. I was a quick study of boardroom gamesmanship and shrewdly made my way up. In time, I was appointed General Manager of a high-profile business with a sizeable staff.

Gazing out my fortieth floor office toward the Statue of Liberty, I reflected on my recent promotion. My effort and sacrifice paid off. I had arrived.

Out of nowhere, a voice welled up from deep within me. The whisper rang with authority, as if directly from my heart.

"Is this all there is?"

I ignored the question, savoring the moment at hand. This position was what I imagined when sweating through exams, late nights in the office, endless flights in a cramped seat eating bad food, and tedious events sucking up to clients. This was my "in your face" to the guys who thought I'd never make it.

"What is the point?"

Man, the new office smell hadn't even worn off!

I had pursued my passion and succeeded. I oversaw hundreds of minions, married a fashion model, and lived in a swank pad on the Upper East Side. I'd never been happier!

Truthfully, my life was not great. The promotion did not fix my problems. Despite a bigger bank account, I didn't sleep better. In fact, I slept less. My work performance still fed my sense of worth. No title, bonus, or accolade quenched my thirst for affirmation and approval. The void inside me grew. At home, life was tense as always. Too many days on the road eroded the foundation of my marriage.

"I still felt empty."

**I dedicated my entire life to a plan that did not deliver.** How was this possible? I worked hard and kept my nose clean. I followed the yellow brick road to success. I even flossed regularly.

Where to now? The *"what"* in my life was obvious. The *"why"* was a mystery.

Almost overnight, the void inside me became a vortex. My zest for achievement wore off, my passion faded. Then, doubt crept in. Fear followed. With despair crouching in the wings, my confidence was shaken.

On the outside, I acted like everything was cool. On the inside, an emotional cancer spread. No business school classes or executive training prepared me for this hopelessness. Seeking help was out of the question. Therapy was for defects, religion for wimps. I had to handle this setback on my own.

My work life deteriorated. I stopped looking up the corporate ladder and stared down. It was a long, long fall. Like a kid stuck in a tree, I grabbed on tight.

The new position was a stretch for me. I wondered whether I could cut it. So did management. With all the relationships I trampled going up, no hearts broke for me on the way down. When they offered me a package, I took their money and left quietly.

My career was rubble. My marriage was dissolving. Then my Mom passed away. The bottom dropped out of my life and I was in a free-fall.

It all happened so fast. I wanted to break out of my funk but felt powerless. The agony was intense. I medicated myself with my usual coping devices: expensive Scotch, porn, and hip clothing. I found no relief.

Like most alpha men, isolation came naturally to me. **I _chose_ to suffer in solitude.** Internalizing my grief or ignoring it complied with the unwritten code of conduct men follow. Our fears or feelings are not common discussion topics at the poker table or over the barbeque.

I didn't have one friend I trusted with my true emotions. I didn't want to be judged or ridiculed. The changes in my life were humiliating and I was ashamed of who I became.

I felt completely alone.

Sounds pathetic, doesn't it? You're probably shaking your head thinking, _This guy is a total loser._ You're right: it was pathetic. My experience is also honest and not unusual.

Guys around us are afflicted with similar feelings of **emptiness, fear, and isolation.** Men at work, friends from home, neighbors, our mechanic, mailman, lawn guy, brothers, and our dads wrestle with these conflicts.

How do I know? I asked.

Over several years, I talked with hundreds of ambitious, competitive alpha men of all vocations, backgrounds, ethnicities, religions, zip codes, and shoe sizes. We tackled issues rarely discussed among one another: purpose, calling, identity, passions, addictions, lusts, girlfriends, wives, fathers, and work.

These were not "I love you, _man!_" gatherings or group hug sessions with a chorus of _Kumbaya._ It was guys like you and me ditching the fake personas and unveiling the reality about who we are. Our dialog was awkward and at times fruitless. We didn't try to fix each other but instead exchanged insights and experiences.

Listening to many alpha men's stories, I was struck by common themes. **There is a collective male experience that remains undisclosed.** Inner conflict strangles us. Frustration and confusion reigns. Weak core values damage our character and compromise our convictions.

The more I investigated, the more troubled I felt about the outlook for our gender. What alarmed me most was that nobody noticed this problem.

## A New Man Code

Why do alpha men crave significance? We yearn "to leave the world a bit better," wrote Ralph Waldo Emerson. Alpha men love acting boldly and courageously, breaking new ground and relentlessly pursuing our mission. Our appetite for innovation inspires others and mobilizes them to make a difference. The thrill of the chase exhilarates us. Burying the competition is even better.

Sadly, highly-charged alpha men are prone to disproportionate disappointment. When we realize conquests do not deliver fulfillment, we grow discouraged. So, we launch new endeavors, experiment, and indulge ourselves. We continue to suffer and despair over setbacks and failures. Unrealized dreams weigh us down. Inside, the pang of emptiness remains. We grow angry and cynical, haunted by the prospect that our life will have less impact than we hoped.

Yet, we never talk about it! **The Alpha Man Code instructs us not to expose our weaknesses and never ask for help.** This unwritten code of behavior is universally accepted despite its questionable principles. This Man Code insists we hide the truth about who we are and what we experience using phrases like "I'm cool" and "It's all good." We try to solve everything on our own. Our attitudes, behaviors, and relationships are tainted by short-sighted strategies worked out in the vacuum of our own mind.

Why are we quiet about this raging conflict inside?

"Look out for Number One" is today's cultural prescription for men's ills. Put Self first. (Self is capitalized because he is *so* important.) Seeking personal glory is not only justifiable—it's encouraged. We crown ourselves king of our empire, worshiping our achievements and their materialistic spoils.

Men can get *exactly* what we want in life and still need more, more, more. Chasing success leaves us exhausted and empty.

Gentlemen, our quest for a meaningful life is futile unless we quit conforming to the shallow, superficial stereotypes defined by the Alpha Man Code. Independence at all cost and self-promotion at any cost do not deliver significance.

**We need a New Man Code that brings out the best in us, not the beast in us.**

## What's In It For Me?

If your life is perfect, do not buy this book! The rest of us cretins need to work to get our act together. Some of us fell into a routine, a rut, or worse. However, a man's life doesn't have to be derailed to benefit from self-examination.

Maybe everything is "fine" for you, yet "fine" feels closer to ordinary than exceptional. Perhaps you have not become the leader or hero you imagined. The trajectory of any man's life can veer off course, falling short of his expectations.

Before we get started, let's get something straight. I don't have an advanced degree in Man-ology or Dude-onomics. No scientific research or double-blind taste tests were conducted. And this is not a Modern Man-ifesto, designed to con or cajole you.

The thoughts put forth in this book are based on my experiences and feedback from hundreds of men I've met. Some of my assertions and generalizations may not square with you. If this annoys you, don't put the book down. Grab a buddy, read the offending line and ask his perspective.

**The point of this book is to challenge men to stop and think about what we believe and why we believe it.**

Our conversation begins with a series of questions, not prepackaged answers. This is not an indictment on the state of men, but an opportunity to strengthen ourselves from the inside. We will pursue authenticity. This search will explore the realities of who we are and the world we inhabit as well as the seeds of discontent, which lie within us. We'll test assumptions and reconsider alpha men's fundamental principles.

As a first step, we will look at the context of our environment and the cultural mandate for men. Next, we will drill down to examine the internal impact, the undisclosed turmoil that hinders our growth. Once we understand the root of our problems, we can explore solutions.

I propose a new vision for men's lives with a compelling standard for us to target. The core of this unique paradigm is heart transformation. The source of power for this change will give us the inner strength to lead effectively in the clutch. Character, influence, and relational excellence will be cornerstones of who we are and how we connect with others.

Such dramatic change requires support from one another. We will discuss how to work together as a body of men, a league of brothers committed to helping one another finish well.

This is not a quick fix, five-step solution with the half-life of a fruit fly. We need substantive, lasting change. Our goal is nothing less than life transformation, radical regeneration from the inside out. Are you up for that?

# Alpha Man vs. God

This level of change starts with a tough decision. **You must choose who has authority in your life.**

Alpha men insist on being in control. Self is our power source. We live by an Alpha Man Code that advocates a reliance on competence, charisma, and individual skills to achieve our personal agenda.

In an alpha man economy, we fight our way to the top and earn others' respect through performance. Results matter, oftentimes defining who we are. Work is a battle to establish where we stand against one another.

This model sustains us on the upswing. However, when we falter such an approach tears us down. Falling short of expectations leaves us riddled with envy or resentment. The ensuing scramble to measure up triggers the dark side of our alpha nature: depravity, depression and addictions.

The Alpha Man Code doesn't allow us to expose our failures and fears. We grit our teeth, "suck it up" and swallow any emotional pain, or we go underground and disconnect from everyone. Sadly, putting on a false front to protect our reputation does little to mitigate the humiliation we feel.

Is this how we want to live?

**There is an alternative: grant God authority in our lives.** Abiding by the will of God rather than our own will is a fundamentally different paradigm from the Alpha Man Code.

We cannot earn God's respect through our achievements. He has a specific mission designed for each of us. This calling leverages our skills to make an impact for Him. Serving and investing in other guys provides the purpose we seek to be men of passion once again.

God knows the truth about us, all our faults and frailties, and yet He accepts us unconditionally. He doesn't condemn us; God restores and redeems us. Regardless of our transgressions, He loves us like sons.

**Whether we believe in God or not, He is with us.** His Spirit walks alongside us, so we are not alone. God does not promise wealth or comfort but rather a life of abundance.

Choosing to build a relationship with God is a matter of faith. We must determine the source of our significance and the basis of real hope: Alpha Man vs. God, Self vs. Spirit.

For many of us, this decision covers new ground. How do we sort out the pros and cons to make a wise judgment? What are the implications? In what ways will we change?

As we explore these options together, we will consider the stories of several alpha men, guys who have walked the same paths as you and me. They re-examined the foundations of their beliefs. God was real and relevant to them. By re-establishing a relationship with God, they experienced redemption and radical change in their lives.

I chose God over Self and my life has transformed.

Serving others and investing in their growth dispels my emptiness. With hope in something eternal, I am liberated from fear. The shackles of shame and guilt are broken. Burdens I harbor are resolved and my anxiety extinguished. And I am no longer alone.

Despite all my mistakes and setbacks, **my life is redeemed**. I experience true joy and my heart is at peace. I am a new man. Gentlemen, you can be too.

# ONE

# Performance Junkies

## The Wounded Get Eaten

The intensity of our professional lives is a product of alpha men's affinity for performance. The upside is recognition, respect, and an enviable lifestyle. However, the downside can be uglier than we realize. Our Alpha Man Code doctrine aggravates our weaknesses and steers us into situations for which we are poorly prepared. The effect on those closest to us can be devastating.

Alpha men want to conquer something big. The competitive pressure of a fierce global marketplace excites us. Alphas are mavericks, independent, innovative and inspirational. We employ dogged means to achieve success, and marshal others to follow our lead.

**Alpha men have a proclivity for performance.** We are hard wired for goals, tasks, and projects. We prefer rules and logic. We base decisions on practiced cost/benefit equations: stock X vs. stock Y, visit a client or powwow with the boss, work out or sleep in, mow the lawn or watch the game.

We track, calculate, compare, and evaluate our actions to establish where we stand compared to others. These self-imposed metrics determine our rank in the pack. Alpha men always want to know where we stand.

We are obsessed by progress rather than process. Results rule. Immediacy is king, and relationships take a back seat. Camaraderie is a victim of getting ahead. Want a friend? Buy a dog!

Alpha men are rarely intimidated by challenges or hurdles. We have great confidence in our ingenuity and ability to overcome obstacles. We believe relentless pursuit of our goals can mask any weakness or flaw.

Time is our most valuable asset and we guard it carefully. To-do lists regulate our lives. Our sense of urgency even impacts our conversations. Men eliminate "unnecessary" details and get straight to the facts. Fix the problem and move ahead—second-guessing is for the meek.

Our business environment is swift and impersonal. There is no room for balance in this heartless arena. Winners are celebrated and losers are cut loose. *Just win baby!* Only speed, intensity and the bottom line are material.

I heard about a sign hung in a Silicon Valley CEO's office that read, "The Weak are Killed. The Wounded are Eaten." Such a ruthlessly efficient workplace can be a slugfest. Day after day we duke it out, bare-knuckled. While we often come out ahead—close the sale, win the bid, reach the quota—the brutality of the battle leaves welts. Make your number and take the spoils. Miss it and get whacked.

The tension of such a life style puts us in a hammerlock before we roll out of bed. The constant grind from morning 'til night, priorities building up, an avalanche of emails: *everybody* wants a piece of us. We expend all our energy to keep work from spinning out of control.

Nobody is immune to a mountain of expectations. As leaders, alpha men wear bull's-eyes on our backs. Sports coaches get axed before the paint dries on their parking space. Twenty-hour days are heralded and "whatever it takes" is barely enough to keep us on the payroll. The tenure of senior executives is getting shorter and shorter. I lasted two years as president of a firm, but I wore a noose around my neck daily. It was not pleasant.

A scene from the movie *Glengarry Glen Ross*[1] depicts this workplace reality. Alec Baldwin, portraying a bombastic executive, gives his team of underperforming salesmen a pep talk. After declaring that coffee was for closers only, he announced to the group, "We're adding something to this month's sales contest. As you all know, first prize is a Cadillac Eldorado. Anyone want to see second prize? Second prize is a set of steak knives. Third prize is you're fired."

Does this sound brutal or familiar? I've heard similar motivational speeches designed to inspire my performance. Making it to the top requires the ABCs Baldwin hammered into his sales guys: **"Always be closing! Always be closing!!"**

It doesn't matter whether we work on Wall Street or Main Street, Broadway or Hollywood, Nashville, Vegas, South Beach or the North Pole: this is the free enterprise system we inhabit.


## I'm Entitled!

Alpha men believe hard work and results warrant rewards. *I've earned this!* Indulging ourselves is justifiable. *I deserve it!* So we buy whatever is necessary to be happy and happening. The better our circumstances, the better we will feel. And life is all about how we feel, right?

Years ago, a buddy recounted a visit to his boss's house for a company function. In a derogatory tone he pronounced, "This guy's place was ten thousand square feet of the most disgusting display of pure opulence and excess I have ever seen." After another sip of his beer, he gazed out the window and continued, "I've *got* to get me one of those."

My friend was afflicted with the latest in designer diseases, Amplified Reference Anxiety. ARA was highlighted in a major newsweekly as a nationwide problem. This malady is "keeping up with the Joneses" on steroids.

Alpha men don't care whether our possessions meet our needs. We stress about how our stuff compares to our neighbors' or the guy in the corner office. **We pine for what we want rather than enjoy what we have**.

Misplaced ambition and achievement-mania often produce arrogance and unhealthy egos. I was a Self-aholic, appointed Chairman of Me, Incorporated. The company slogan was "Love Thyself" and my mission was simple: the unadulterated pursuit of status and net worth for yours truly. Get to the top by any means possible and feel free to indulge along the way.

Such a self-aggrandizing perspective is not uncommon. In the premiere edition of his men's magazine *Sly* Sylvester Stallone preached, "Gorge yourself at the banquet of life until the only thing left on the table are crumbs." This high-octane lifestyle is attractive yet treacherous.

The ancient Israeli leader Haggai conveyed the limitations of allowing greed to displace meaning: "You have planted much but have harvested little. You eat but never have enough. You drink, but never have your fill. You put on clothes but are not warm. You earn wages only to put them in a purse with holes."[2]

Current research supports the Jewish prophet over the Italian Stallion. A study from the University of Illinois concluded that members of the Forbes 400 were only slightly happier than the public as a whole. *Time Magazine* confirmed this inherent fact of humanity, reporting, "There is no significant relationship between how much money a person earns and whether he or she feels good about life."[3]

If our accomplishments don't make us happier, why do we sacrifice our family life, compromise our character and cede self-respect to become wealthier or cooler than others? There is no logic or reason in that equation.

# One Man's Story

*Doug was a performance junkie. Growing up in Idaho, he was a two sport standout in high school and landed a Division I baseball scholarship. While his college teammates became household names in the majors, Doug went into business.*

*His career took off. By the time Doug was in his thirties, he was CEO of a technology company. He was highly respected in his field and sought after by head hunters for top posts. With a promising professional future, beautiful wife, fabulous apartment, and three lovely children enrolled in Manhattan's most prestigious prep schools, life seemed grand. Doug was happy.*

*Pressure at work, though, went home with him. Eventually, he took it out on his family. When his wife complained, he sought refuge at a local pub, downing pints and chatting up waitresses. He deserved some relief. As his strain at the office and stress at home grew, his benders became more frequent and his excuses less viable. Then, he turned to drugs.*

*When I first met Doug, he was cheerful and confident, certain he had his life under control. The signs of desperation were unmistakable. Doug was in denial about how his work aspirations impacted himself and his family. "I'm not such a bad guy," Doug insisted to me. With a newborn in her arms, his wife rolled her eyes as he rationalized his behavior. "Compared to others, I'm a decent husband."*

*Doug muted his guilt by blaming his wife. "She's constantly carping on me. She's not holding up her end of the deal." Dismissing her feelings and deflecting culpability were evidence of a man unwilling to deal with the reality of his own flaws and mistakes—typical alpha man behavior.*

*Then the train wreck happened. Doug's wife locked him out of their apartment. She filed for divorce and police protection. Accusations flew. His wife refused child visitation rights, and closed their bank accounts. Doug slept on a buddy's couch and borrowed money to stay afloat.*

*Doug suffered intense pain. He missed his kids and his wife. Doug missed his life. He hit bottom. The speed of his fall shocked him.* **Doug wanted to master the universe, but couldn't master himself.**

*"I just wish I had some hope," he wept. Doug would have done* anything *to regain his family.*

---

Doug possessed the intelligence and drive to build businesses. Unfortunately, he did not apply the same vigor to other parts of his life. He figured performance at work and the right lifestyle would cover up his inadequacies as husband and father. A string of achievements did not grant him immunity to setbacks or emotional anguish. Doug's suffering demonstrated the reality of being a one-dimensional man obsessed with his personal agenda.

## The Unwritten Code

Alpha men are not oblivious to the impact of our quest to be the best. We recognize there are consequences of our fanatical ambition and self-interest. So why do we continue to chase success without accurately assessing the cost?

Cultural definitions of manhood contribute to our miscalculation. In fact, an unwritten code of conduct has influenced men for generations. This Alpha Man Code schooled every guy I've known since we were kids, regardless of background, education or ethnicity.

Do any of the following sound familiar?

- Walk it off  (Dealing with physical injury)
- Keep cool  (Dealing with emotional injury)
- Don't rat on your buddies  (Dealing with perjury)
- Suck it up  (Dealing with persecution)
- Every Man for Himself  (Dealing with the world)
- Hide your weaknesses  (Dealing with other men)
- Boys will be boys  (Dealing with women)
- Never ask for help  (Dealing with the unknown)
- Don't be a wuss  (Dealing with risk)
- Don't admit your failures  (Dealing with reality)

Where did you first hear these tenets—fifth grade recess? Uncle Bob? How did you scrutinize their validity? If the Alpha Man Code is as dopey as the He-Man Woman Haters Club, why do so many men still cave in to it?

Who composed the Alpha Man Code? Was it scratched out on the back of a game program or a bar napkin? How was it ratified? Is it kept in some underground vault or an ancient tabernacle?

The Alpha Man Code preaches self-sufficiency. This angle pits us against the world. Don't trust anyone; don't count on others; never commit unless you're out of options.

**Self is the source of an alpha man's strength.** We are at war with authority. According to Alpha Man Code doctrine, we are masters of our destiny. We want control at all times. If possible, be in command. Submitting to the will of others is for sheep.

At work, following the code means we are better individual producers than team players. We rely on our own smarts and determination as the best chance for success. While we welcome any task, we are not interested in any advice. We are strong-willed leaders with all the answers. When facing setbacks or errors in our judgment, we grind it out rather than admit culpability or solicit help.

Our behavior at home is much the same. We can be active in our family life but not engaged. Playing the part of husband and father is easier than giving ourselves over completely. Intimacy is difficult to achieve when we are unwilling to reveal our deepest fears or regrets. When conflict arises, it's never our fault. We believe we are always right.

**The Alpha Man Code doesn't define manhood, it hides truth.** With a twisted sense of virility, the code suggests we cover up our shortcomings, inadequacies, and emotional wounds. The Alpha Man Code is a mask we wear because we are afraid of being exposed. Instead of addressing problems, we allow them to fester in the dark. Our reputation is more important than our reality.

## One Man's Story

*Billy, a TV news anchor, was a disciple of the Alpha Man Code. His boyhood motto was "always be calm, cool and collected." School, sports, and social life came easily for him. Billy grew increasingly independent and self-sufficient, never needing anyone's help.*

*Professionally, success started for Billy after his first career change. At a New York consulting firm, his column in a travel trade publication enhanced his industry status and quickened his advancement. Soon he was heading a new division.*

*"I got plenty of press and the business was ready to explode," Billy recalled, "but I was miserable." As a young executive, he was uncertain how to lead most effectively. "I needed help to get to the next level but was afraid to ask."*

*Acting like a rock on the outside did not eliminate trembling on the inside. Underneath Billy's Alpha Man*

*Code demeanor, fear and insecurity reigned. When he developed an ulcer in his twenties Billy realized he suffered a physical toll burying his emotional strife.*

*Soliciting assistance might have launched his company and remedied his leadership gaps. Instead of facing his shortcomings, Billy moved on.*

*After enrolling in broadcast journalism classes at Columbia University, he took non-paid internships in radio and television news. His demeanor and flawless elocution enabled him to land a coveted anchor position. Once again, he beat the odds and launched a successful new career.*

*Despite all Billy's professional triumphs and personal excesses he experienced, something was missing in his life. "I was totally self-reliant, all determination and no dependence. And it wasn't working."*

*At 31, Billy hit a wall. Standing on a subway platform, he questioned whether he mattered at all. "If I jumped in front of a train, would anyone care?" Billy wasn't suicidal, just astray. Throughout his life, he was running or hiding, fearful his limitations would be revealed.*

Billy fell victim to an Alpha Man Code focused on how we look and who we know rather than who we are and what we believe. Sadly, too many of us suffer the same.

Performance junkies can make an impact; unfortunately, the collateral damage to our selves and those around us can last a lifetime. This is not an isolated problem, but one that affects men across generations, vocations, ethnicities, and religions.

Ironically, alpha men strive for individual success while failing collectively: we remain beholden to a cultural doctrine we did not design or approve. Many of us are blind to the consequences of living according to the Alpha Man Code. The rest of us seem too selfish to lend a hand.

I am sure you can see the effect on others. Can you feel the impact on yourself?

# TWO

# Men of Mediocrity

## Stagnated Growth

None of us said, "When I grow up, I want to be third-stringer." "Mommy, I want to be known as someone who chokes in the clutch," or "I hope my career starts out with a bang and ends with a whimper."

While these statements don't represent our dreams, they often become our reality. Abiding by a code of conduct designed to cover up our flaws results in dysfunction. Generations of men experience early success in their lives only to see it fade. Trudging through years of routine without rich meaning leaves us passionless and apathetic.

In the movie *Fight Club*[4] Brad Pitt plays Tyler Durden, an eclectic leader who taps into guys' empty lives through an underground fight club. In a speech to the group, he weighs in on the state of men:

"I see all this potential and I see it squandered. An entire generation pumping gas, waiting tables...slaves in white collars. Advertising has us chasing cars and clothes, working in jobs we hate so we can buy stuff we don't need....

"We're the middle children of history, no purpose or place. We have no Great War. No Great Depression. Our Great War is a spiritual war. Our Great Depression is our lives.

13

"We're all raised on television to believe one day, we'd all be millionaires and movie gods and rock stars. But we won't. We're slowly learning that fact. And, we're very pissed off."

Durden strikes a chord. Men are slaves to our own desires. Cars and clothes and dreams of glory distract us from greatness. **Men are mired in mediocrity. We seem content being average.** We're intense and competitive in some areas of our lives and slackers in others. We fritter away great potential through sloppy and reckless behavior. At work, we compromise our principles to put up the numbers and get ahead. The easy road is chosen over the hard path. Shrewdness and guile are used to stretch the rules rather than relying on character to stay within bounds. The consequences to others seem irrelevant, as long as we move ahead.

At home, we are no better. Instead of battling to resolve family challenges, we pay lawyers wads of cash to unravel us from obligations. Generations of kids suffer because we lack the backbone to keep marriages functional and together, or we abandon children sired out of wedlock. Is this the example we want our children to follow?

If the GM of our favorite team announced his goal was to be perpetually middle of the pack, fans would revolt. Nobody wants to work for a firm that aspires to be just average.

**Men's growth stagnates due to lack of commitment to excellence in three areas: our character, personal accountability, and relationships.** Unless we apply our best efforts to improve these facets, many of us will settle for lives smaller than we dreamed.


## Character Flaws

The problem for alpha men is that achievement at work is more than our livelihood; it is our lifestyle. We love power. It is essential to our Man Code persona. However, when our authority is threatened we grow anxious. Our strengths can become weaknesses.

Loss of control made me a micromanager, impatient with people, and intolerant of failure. My drive to succeed turned into domination, my sense of competition into combativeness, and my intensity into intimidation. Expectations for others—and my self—became unrealistic. I blamed others while refusing to admit my mistakes.

If our authority fades, alpha men try harder and harder to prove our worth. The big bonus enables us to one-up our neighbor with a McMansion, a Hummer, and a 100-inch HDTV. Soon, we don't want a promotion, we *need* one to cover the mortgage and maxed-out credit cards. This leveraged position has a big downside.

Anyone's career can hit a pothole, taking us from hero to zero overnight. The first place we crack is our character. Moral standards sag, and integrity is negotiable. As pressure builds, our values and convictions crumble. Our competitive nature blinds us to consequences as we try to claw our way back on top.

Too often, **cutting corners is the magical solution**. Hemingway wrote, "All things truly wicked start from innocence."[5] A small fudge here, a short cut there—in the beginning, nobody plans to rip off clients or swindle shareholders. Situations deteriorate and our relentless nature leads to compromises of integrity as acceptable means of fixing our problems. The collateral damage can be devastating.

Is the explosion of corporate corruption an aberration or a by-product of a survival-of-the-fittest mentality where ends justify means? Does no holds barred translate to no boundaries? Is it a crime if you don't get caught?

A trader told me there are two truths on Wall Street: everyone lies, and everyone lies *all* the time. Whether this is true or just part of the gamesmanship of the profession, being a man of your word is tough amongst such rampant deceit.

In his book *The Cheating Culture,* David Callahan exposes dishonesty everywhere. Half of all resumes include lies. Padding expense reports, looting office supplies closets, fudging taxes, pirating music and cable TV, and ripping off insurance companies have become commonplace. Eighty percent of executives Callahan surveyed admitted to cheating at golf.

**Alpha men worry less about what is right or wrong than about what we can get away with.** This tolerant attitude is fine until we send a loved one under the knife of a doctor who faked his way through med school. Are we confident with representation by a lawyer who cheated on his Bar exam? What compromises are made by the guy investing our kid's college fund or the dude fixing our brakes?

## Lack of Accountability

Not all our transgressions are public. We keep much of our personal life private from others. We offer little visibility into our relationships with women, management of our finances, or emotional travails. This lack of personal accountability contributes to our inconsistent conduct.

An old business saying goes, without accountability there is mediocrity. Companies cannot grow unless systems of fiduciary control and individual accountability are in place. These processes are second nature to us.

Where are these systems in our personal life? Bosses and shareholders make us stick to sales quotas but no one holds us to our marital vows. Clients assess our business promises with quality standards yet our personal promises have no warranty.

**Lack of accountability in our personal lives strangles men's development**. Over the years, coaches, professors and bosses challenged us to stretch our talents. Who calls us out now? Who pushes back when we cut corners?

Any man can be caught in a bad place at a weak moment. Resisting temptation or destructive habits is too difficult to tackle on our own. **To grow emotionally and spiritually, men need a high level of transparency with other men.** Granting visibility into dark areas of our life is critical, yet rarely practiced.

## One Man's Story

*John is a successful Wall Street advisor, and invests his free time serving at a homeless shelter. He often stays overnight to ensure men there are safe and cared for. Not long ago, John spent his nights in a jail cell.*

*Growing up in the Midwest, John had big plans. His father, a fighter pilot in the Air Force, was the first African American to own a Gulf station in Cleveland. John admired his father's diligence and envisioned grand accomplishments. Despite limited athletic ability, he "longed, yearned, burned for a football scholarship to college."*

*Hard work and an obsession to succeed paid off when he landed a spot at a Division I-AA football powerhouse in the Northeast. This accomplishment reinforced John's confidence in his self-sufficiency.*

*With such a strong will, a few mind-altering drugs seemed harmless. John easily justified this illicit activity. He didn't need accountability on this decision. John established his own theology, "one in which drugs, alcohol and sexual promiscuity were permissible as long as they were pursued like a gentleman."*

*After graduation, he bulked up to take a run at the NFL. The competition was brutal. As dreams of a sports career faded, his addictions grew. Drinking led to binging, and then cocaine. Though his guile propelled him through graduate school and a string of solid jobs, John left a trail of broken promises and shattered relationships. He landed in jail—not once or twice—over thirty times. When bailed out, he always pledged to change.*

*John's determination was not enough to overcome his addictions. The downward spiral continued as he refused to solicit help. "Most sad was my acceptance of the unacceptable—living in my offices when crack cocaine took away the ability to maintain a place of my own. I went from a 250-pound linebacker to a 165-pound weakling whose skin always itched."*

*A drug possession charge and probation violations landed him in county lock-up for a month. He faced more serious charges if he did not get his act together.*

*Despite mounting evidence to the contrary, John still believed he had the will power to pull himself out of his nosedive. He resisted giving others full visibility into his world and half-heartedly considered their advice. John insisted he had all the answers.*

---

Personal accountability does not just happen: a man must make a conscious decision to appoint someone to fill the role. Then, one must be willing to deal with the truth about who we are and accept wise counsel for changes we must enact.

Inviting others into flawed regions of our lives is scary and threatening. This is especially true in our relationships, an area where many of us feel inept.

## Transactional Relationships

The Alpha Man Code teaches us that relationships are means to an end. Connections with others are stepping-stones to our goals, necessary evil to treat with caution. Family and friends will let you down, colleagues will betray you, and women will eat you alive. Be guarded with commitment and *always* have an escape route.

Relationships are messy and cumbersome. Alpha men often apply limited effort to maintain them. Relationships run counter to our preference for tangible goals. Intimacy makes us squeamish. Communication is a weakness for guys, particularly with women.

One common solution is both predictable and nonsensical: "If I just find the right woman, I'll be happy." Is relational day trading the answer? "If my business partner were better, I'd be successful." Will our flaws disappear if we work with someone else? "If only there was a company which truly appreciated me." We seldom identify the need for change in our half of a relationship.

A workplace performance mentality is hard to turn off when we head home. The thirst for results bleeds into our family life. We compare our kids advancement to others: Jack Jr. walked at nine months; Jenny got all A's; Frankie made quarterback on the football team.

Asking "What have you done for me lately?" in a family scenario means love for our kids is conditional. Is it possible our attention must be earned? Could quality time be divvied up based on Bobby's baseball performance or Ruthie's report card? Ask your kids what it's like measuring up to your standards. As alpha dads, both judgmental and self-righteous, we push our kids for results instead of encouraging them with love and forgiveness.

Conditional marriages are commonplace. Nowadays, "till death do us part" can mean "for the foreseeable future." So often men's commitments amount to "I'll be the husband I'm supposed to be *only* if you are the wife you are supposed to be." This is not a formula for a loving relationship: it's an economic exchange.

**Performance junkies don't build relationships, we conduct transactions.** Men don't communicate with others, we negotiate. Love is a chit to get sex. Friendship is a means of moving to the front of the line. Teamwork lasts as long as it is win–win. We always seek an edge, angling to come out on top. People become commodities we trade to further our agenda, or worse yet, a sport to keep us entertained.

For years, **the foundation of my relationships was what I could get rather than what I could give.** I used people for my own gain. To protect myself, each relationship was fitted with a nifty exit strategy so I could move on when something better came along. Commitment is hard to establish when "no strings attached" is a prerequisite.

In *The Godfather*, Don Corleone offered this advice: "A man who doesn't spend time with his family can never be a real man."[6] Do we waste too much mindshare on our professional leadership aspirations? How much thought should we apply to being a loving husband or father?

I believe any guy is capable of building intimate, lasting and fulfilling relationships. Men can root for a favorite team through even the hardest times. I have been a member of the Red Sox Nation living in New York. I suffered through torturous seasons yet I *never* considered becoming a Yankee fan. Our families deserve this level of commitment.

A friend had a favorite saying when it came to relationships. "Smitty," he'd say, clapping me on the shoulder, "They're *all* good in the beginning." He hit it spot on. **Alpha men lack relational stamina.** Our conditioning sucks! When immediate results falter, we grow weary. We're winded by communication. Getting to know someone wears us out. The emotional rollercoaster leaves us gasping.

Unfortunately, alpha men are reluctant to commit enough time or effort to build relational excellence. We do not tenaciously develop our relationships despite knowing they're vital to our well being.

Many have tried self-help solutions, quick fixes for our behaviors and actions. However, this approach only treats the symptoms. Self-serving motivations and attitudes remain in place.

To experience real growth, we have to look below the surface. Embarking on this self-examination is new for many alpha men but the results can be life-changing.

# THREE

# Undisclosed Conflict

## Chasing After the Wind

"For the secret of a man's being is not only to live...but to live for something definite," wrote the Russian novelist Dostoevsky in *The Brothers Karamazov.* "Without a firm notion of what he is living for, man will not accept life and would rather destroy himself than remain on earth."

In my discussions with hundreds of guys through ministry and research for this book, I found that inner conflict is universal. Even the most powerful men wrestle with undisclosed internal chaos. **Emptiness, fear, and isolation affect all men at critical seasons in our lives.**

Loathe to admit any weakness, we allow these maladies to linger. We ignore emptiness, deny fear, and cover up our isolation. Eventually, these burdens seep into our motivations and attitudes, impacting our actions and behaviors. The damage manifests in our relationships at work and at home.

In a *60 Minutes* interview,[7] three-time Super Bowl winner Tom Brady made a startling comment. He has won most valuable player awards, signed multi-million dollar contracts, and is lock for the Hall of Fame admission. Endorsing products on TV, dating supermodels, and hosting *Saturday Night Live,* Brady lives the life many men crave. When asked to reflect on his accomplishments, he stared blankly at the camera. "God, it's got to be more than this," Brady said in a melancholy tone. "I mean this can't be what it's all cracked up to be."

How could championship rings, the respect of his peers, adulation of fans, money, and women fail to fill the void within this high-achieving alpha man?

Solomon, the ancient Israeli king and wealthiest, most powerful leader of his time, expressed a similar sentiment in his memoir *Ecclesiastes*. Solomon was Bill Gates times ten; he invented the rock star lifestyle, and made Wilt Chamberlain seem like a choir boy. "I denied myself nothing my eyes desired; I refused my heart no pleasure," he wrote. "Yet when I surveyed all that my hands had done and what I had toiled to achieve, everything was meaningless, a chasing after the wind."[8]

Why do alpha men separated by thousands of years experience the same sense of emptiness? Why is this feeling of futility so familiar to many of us?

In *The Unheard Cry for Meaning,* renowned psychologist and concentration camp survivor Victor Frankl wrote, "Ever more people today have the means to live, but no meaning to live for."[9] **Men can set goal after goal to answer "What next?" but we can't answer "Why?"**

Nietzsche mused, "He who has a why to live for can bear almost any how." Purpose is the "why" in our lives. Without purpose, we simply exist. Without purpose, we are directionless and unfocused, bobbing along on the whims of circumstance. Without purpose, men can achieve what we desire most and *still* feel unfulfilled.

What is our purpose? How do we find our calling?

With the words "It's not about you," Rick Warren opens his best-seller *The Purpose Driven Life.* Warren posits that **Self is our central problem:** "The purpose of your life is far greater than your own personal fulfillment, your peace of mind or even your happiness. It's far greater than your family, your career or even your wildest dreams and ambitions."[10]

Why do alpha men struggle understanding purpose? According to Warren, "We ask self-centered questions like, 'What do I want to be? What should I do with my life? What are my goals, my ambitions, my dreams for my future?' But focusing on ourselves will never reveal life's purpose."

Leaders must consider how we apply our skills, relationships, finances, and time on endeavors more profound than a self-serving agenda. Frankl tells us, "For success, like happiness, cannot be pursued, it must ensue, and it only does so as the unintended side-effect of one's personal dedication to a cause greater than oneself or as the by-product of one's surrender to a person other than oneself."

For Alpha Man Code devotees, surrendering to someone else is the ultimate sin. Self-centeredness held me captive. In order to change my long-term strategy I have to give up my self-focused worldview. I was afraid.

Fear complicates men's struggle with emptiness. Refusing to examine ourselves, our views and assumptions prevent us from developing fully.


## Imprisoned by Fear

Alpha men are supposed to be fearless. According to our code, a real man overflows with machismo and is immune to insecurity and doubt. Nothing cracks our armor of confidence. We charge into each day willing to slay whatever stands in our way.

When was the last time an alpha guy made any of these statements?

- "Hey Bob, I'm feeling a little vulnerable at work."
- "I'll tell you Josh, I don't think the money I stashed away is enough to retire."
- "If my girlfriend knew the real me, she won't like what she saw."

- "Ya know Joe, maybe I *am* inadequate as a husband and father."
- "Truthfully Steve, I don't have a clue where my life is headed."

We never declare these sentiments, but that doesn't mean we never feel them. Fear can start small. Indecision and impatience crop up. Obstacles grow in size. Setbacks seem monumental. Down seasons feel permanent. We become obsessed with opposition, consumed by what could go wrong rather than what could go right.

Fear is devious and deceptive, hiding in the shadows as if it doesn't exist. We gloss over this emotion, unwilling to acknowledge its foothold. Fear gathers strength in the darkness.

This is not an attack by the Boogie Man. It is a hijacking of the mind and soul. Fear rattles the depths of our being: **fear of failure, fear of rejection, fear of inadequacy, and fear of insignificance.**

Though we deny fear's impact, savvy marketers make big money on it. Viagra sales don't lie. Ads promoting products as "strong and lasting" play on our fear of being weak and impotent. TV hawks ten-ton trucks for when we don't feel rugged, cologne for when we don't feel suave, and high-tech athletic shoes to distract attention from our kegger bellies.

A few years back, I was on my way to lunch with a partner of a prominent Wall Street firm. He was a stately fellow, polished and confident, with a six-figure salary, four-bedroom apartment, and three daughters. It was a sweltering summer day, and he wore a suit and tie.

"So what's the dress code at your firm on Fridays?" I asked.

"Business casual," he replied, squinting into the sun as we crossed the street, "unless you are meeting with a client."

"When's your client meeting?"

"None today," he replied matter-of-factly. "Don't want to look like I don't have clients."

I was dumbfounded by his behavior. If an executive at that level could be intimidated by others' opinions, the implications for peons below him were dire.

In its most insidious form, fear turns our actions into our identity: I didn't just lose that one account, I'm a flop; I didn't just avoid the conflict, I'm a coward; I didn't just split up with her, I'm unwanted; I didn't just party too hard last night, I'm a drunk. When we label ourselves out of fear, it's difficult to untangle ourselves from that identity.

## One Man's Story

*No one is impervious to fear. Consider the following episode told by Dr. Martin Luther King. The situation he describes happened during his early activity in the civil rights movement when his coalition began to fracture and his family was in harm's way:*

*"I got out of bed and began to walk the floor...I was ready to give up. With my cup of coffee sitting untouched before me I tried to think of a way to move out of the picture without appearing a coward. In this state of exhaustion, when my courage had all but gone, I decided to take my problem to God. With my head in my hands, I bowed over the kitchen table and prayed aloud. The words I spoke to God that midnight are still in my memory. "I am here taking a stand for what I believe is right. But now, **I am afraid.** The people are looking to me for leadership and if I stand before them without strength and courage, they too will falter. I am at the end of my powers. I have nothing left. I've come to the point where I cannot face it alone."[11]*

*His brilliant speeches provided inspiration for millions yet like many of us Dr. King struggled with insecurity.*

Fear can arrest any man. A buddy bugged me for weeks to catch up over coffee. He was a successful entrepreneur and on his way to the altar. We scheduled times, but he cancelled again and again. Eventually, we huddled in a conference room over a cup of Joe.

He cracked jokes to relieve his tension. It was clear he had something serious on his mind. I tried to make him feel at ease, but he broke down. He mashed his tears with his thumb and forefinger and apologized. My mind raced. *Did he lose a fortune in the market? Was the IRS after him?*

"I've been trying to talk to you but never found the courage," he sobbed. His body heaved with emotion. I was scared. *Was his fiancé pregnant? Did he have cancer?* Ten minutes passed before he gathered enough composure to speak clearly.

"I've been hiding something for years," he said through his tears. "I'm hooked on pornography." Shame gushed out of him. Fear of exposing this secret held him hostage. As I assured him the worst was over, I realized the power fear can have over men.

Perhaps we are courageous enough to run into a burning building, but could we tell a friend about a gambling problem or a drug habit? We might have the boldness to execute a risky deal but do we have the wherewithal to tell our wife about the gentlemen's club we frequent? Will we have the guts to tell our sons how frightened we are to make the same mistakes as our fathers?

We can't avoid or eliminate fear: we must face it.

While concerns about our future or our current situation are scary, nothing frightens us more than the reality of our own carnal nature. On the surface, we consider ourselves decent guys trying to do the right thing. We might stumble during a weak moment, but we're not bad men. Prisons house all the bad men.

The Russian author Aleksandr Solzhenitsyn points out the naiveté of this viewpoint. In *The Gulag Archipelago* he wrote, "If only there were evil people somewhere insidiously committing evil deeds, and it were necessary only to separate them from the rest of us and destroy them. But **the line dividing good and evil cuts through the heart of every human being."**12

Solzhenitsyn makes a profound point: the world is not segregated into good guys and bad guys. All men are inherently flawed. This is the frailty of our humanity. Each of us has a corrupt heart. We are not so different from steroid users, corporate swindlers, or corrupt politicians. We judge them because they cross legal lines and get caught yet we cross lines of morality, decency, and justice in our private lives. We know it is wrong, but we can't stop ourselves.

This is the root of our fear: we are petrified our depravity will overtake us and be exposed. The light of truth will reveal who we really are. Others will be appalled. Loved ones will turn away. Not only will we be humiliated, we will be condemned and scorned.

Many men hide in fear, and we do so alone.

## Nocturnal Hearts

Men romanticize the cowboy. We love his rugged individualism, a man capable and comfortable by himself on the expanse of the open range. Men dream of such freedom and independence. However, the hombre on the plains is not far from the loner of the old country western songs wailing, "My dog died, my wife left me, so I'm alone and I'm drinkin' again."

**Isolation is bred into us.** Looking out for number one is the Alpha Man Code paradigm for getting ahead. Autonomy is vital to compete in our eat-or-be-eaten environment. We prefer making the daily kill without anyone's help.

As challenges with work or relationships confront us, men disconnect rather than engage others in solving the problem. We retreat. Feelings, fears and failures are soft spots in need of protection. We learn to hide experiences that drape us in shame, mistakes that plague us with guilt, injustices we resent, iniquities we endure, and coping devices we employ.

Our hearts are nocturnal, only exposed when we are certain it is safe. Much of the cover-up espoused by the Alpha Man Code attempts to protect our hearts from external danger.

Independence is the path of least resistance (and the least emotional risk). It is more comfortable to process our conflicts in the privacy of our own mind, or put off thinking about them at all. Autonomous decisions don't require anyone's consent. There's little risk we'll have to acknowledge our faults. What we think needs to be buried stays buried.

There is a fine line between solitude and loneliness. Men choose solitude. We fall into loneliness. Solitude involves self-reflection; it can be constructive and rejuvenating. Loneliness results from pushing others away, and leads to self-pity.

Loneliness isn't the result of a lack of companionship. Men's camaraderie with one another can perpetuate loneliness. What we call friendships are no more than acquaintances; superficial, and void of vulnerability or candor. The Alpha Man Code prohibits digging too deep into one another's private world. While buddies may glimpse a facet or two, we prevent anyone from seeing the full picture.

Most men have only a handful of friends we trust with our deepest concerns, fears or regrets. Sadly, as we age this circle gets smaller. **Lack of true friendships is why so many men are plagued by the conflicts below the surface.**

Going it alone in life is not daring or adventuresome, it's foolish and cowardly. Without accountability in our lives, blind spots can be deadly. We lack objectivity. Circular logic abounds, and we ruminate and rationalize away responsibility. We let ourselves off easy or punish ourselves without mercy.

As an Army of One, we have no wingman. Nobody has our back.

# One Man's Story

*Seth is an engineer for a multinational corporation. He recently married and lives in a new suburban home. His family life today is joyful, a significant change from his upbringing.*

*He grew up with a turbulent, alcoholic father. When Seth's dad was fired from his job and arrested due to drinking, Seth's mother provided for the family. Even with her income, they needed food stamps, then welfare to survive.*

*Kids at school mocked Seth. Though a strong student, his shame was so overwhelming he was afraid to speak in class. "I felt lonely and incompetent so I isolated myself."*

*Seth hoped college would provide an escape from his adolescent strife. He focused on his studies and was accepted at a top university. Even at this high point in a hard life, Seth was haunted by internal pain. Academic achievement couldn't mend childhood wounds and dysfunctional relationships.*

*With so much internal turmoil, Seth flunked out of college. Promising to pull himself together and go back to school, he took a day laborer job. A year passed, then five, then seven.*

*Seth maintained a friendly demeanor that hid his emotional seclusion. A low-risk lifestyle provided the control he desired to protect his tender psyche. Seth fell into comfortable routines and predictable patterns of behavior.*

*He kept his circle of friends at arm's length. His relationships with women were infrequent and rarely intimate. Constantly checking his emotions exhausted him. Seth desperately wanted help but was too ashamed to ask for it. Shutting others out of his life left him with nobody to turn to.*

Seth's isolation was incapacitating, and unfortunately, not unusual. You don't have to face childhood trauma to struggle like him. Albert Einstein said, "It's strange to be known universally and yet to be so lonely." James Dean, the 1950s screen idol, called acting the loneliest profession in the world.

Many guys express similar sentiments. Successful, active in their community, loaded with friends and family, **men can be surrounded by people yet feel alone.**

When I separated from my ex-wife, I desperately wanted to share my burdens with somebody. Instead, I covered up the truth about my failing marriage and hid in a downtown apartment. For six months, I fended off inquiries, acting like everything was normal. I hoped somebody would ask the extra question, to get past my defense mechanisms, and probe for the real issues burdening my heart. Even dropping hints didn't entice others to take the bait.

Sadly, our friends and family are often too distracted by their own lives or can't be bothered to help us. Some try to fix us with a get-tough remedy. Others consider us contagious and jet. And there we are, alone again.

"Life is full of misery, loneliness and suffering," quipped Woody Allen. "And it's all over much too soon."

Alpha men are more optimistic about our future but our confident demeanor does not protect us from emotional pain. We can have a string of accomplishments yet still be plagued by instability inside. Emptiness, fear and isolation can be debilitating.

The root of this inner conflict is a heart deficit. There is a gulf in our core that we try to fill with positions and possessions. Nothing works. The path to resolving our heart deficit starts by addressing several unanswered questions.

# FOUR

# Foundational Questions

## Who am I?

There is a joke in which a pilot announces to his passengers, "I have good news and bad news. The bad news is we are lost. The good news is we are making *great* time!"

Alpha men speed through life striving to perform better and accomplish more. Unfortunately, we don't scrutinize where we are headed or why we are going there. In our rush for results, we lose our bearings and find ourselves reacting to the chaos around us.

In leadership roles, we know the best way to get a project back on track is to ask great questions. We are skilled at ferreting out underlying issues, testing assumptions and researching market needs in order to make wise choices. Too bad we don't apply this same model to our personal situation.

Who am I? What do I believe? Do I count? Where do I stand? Answers to these foundational questions can re-establish purpose and put us on a clear path to our future. These answers will affect our attitudes and motivations. As we explore these questions we will better understand our core values and the source of our hope and faith.

Examining these questions will lead us into the Alpha Man vs. God debate and provide the groundwork for recapturing our passion for life. Gentlemen, let's not waste any more time.

How do you define yourself? Write down a sentence describing who you are. Don't groan and roll your eyes. Grab a pen. Use the margins of this page and get started. Take your time, I'll wait.

Finished? Great. Does the description reflect your career situation, family ties, or personal passions? Could it apply to you at any time in your life? Would your answer cause friends and family to nod their heads or laugh out loud?

What is the source of your identity?

**Too often, alpha men define our selves by performance or expertise:** I'm Lance the Lawyer, I'm Carl the Big Deal Closer, I'm Mitch the Platinum Album Musician. "What do you do?" is a basic introductory pleasantry between two guys. *(Funny, I rarely answer, "I'm Dave the Great Dad.")* To gain credibility, we rattle off our educational pedigree, professional accomplishments and network of affiliations designed to differentiate ourselves as winners and somebodys.

If the source of our identity is externally defined, we are at the mercy of the material world. Circumstances change. Marketplace fluctuations, the whims of nature and the fickleness of mankind can tear us apart if we rely on results to establish who we are.

---

## One Man's Story

*As part of the Hollywood inner circle, Jered was a guest at backyard barbeques of Oscar-winning actors. He clubbed with celebutants and hung out at intimate gatherings of movie moguls.*

*His L.A. lifestyle was a far cry from his upbringing in Tulare, a sleepy California farming town. Because he believed his identity was defined by a place nobody recognized, Jered felt like a nobody.*

*Desperate to be known and accepted, Jered moved to Los Angeles to try acting. He connected with promoters and infiltrated the exclusive West Hollywood nightclub scene.*

*Association was the local narcotic and Jered learned how to deal. "Being attached to celebrities was power you couldn't buy." The more friendships Jered built, the more sought-after he became, particularly among the influential gay community. "I used my body as a lure to get into parties and mingle with celebrities," he said. "I was able to call home and boast about hanging with somebody famous."*

*Maintaining an image meant Jered assumed the labels others bestowed on him. Jered gained status and wealth. People were drawn to him. At 22, Jered had a new identity: he was an L.A. player.*

*His popularity did not quell his internal craving. He needed more and more. The speed of his lifestyle took its toll. Jered hit bottom on an evening out with a buddy. "It was a night filled with clubbing, drinking, cocaine, and topped with black tar heroine to come down. After I passed out, my friend molested me."*

*Jered was haunted by that evening. His identity was screwed up and his psyche permanently scarred. "I sold out my soul to be in the same room with a celebrity." He realized the consequences of defining himself by such superficial measures.*

Jered's story is extreme. However, it's not so different from our own. Alpha men construct identities through association with others. We use external markers to define ourselves. In the process, many of us sell our soul for the right firm, job title, or address. We live for a label rather than fulfill a calling.

Maybe you are thinking, *"That's not me. I don't care what others think. I define my identity on my own terms."* Really? Let's be honest: it is difficult to avoid defining who we are by our accomplishments, associations, or affinities (NY Giants fan, Red Sox Nation). Any of these materialistic measures can become yesterday's news or last year's model. We need our identity built on something more stable, a source which is eternal.

**God is eternal.** We can define who we are based on our relationship with Him. This is a radical yet practical approach. To explore this concept, we need to be certain of what we believe.

## What Do We Believe?

Before committing to a mortgage, we devote hundreds of hours and thousands of dollars on expert advice. The size of an investment and the long-term implications demand due diligence. Have we invested the proper amount of time to determine if God exists? Have we researched the evidence thoroughly? Do we know for certain what our final destination will be?

Some of us ascribe to a secular worldview. Life is random. We are nothing more than a cosmic accident. Luck is part of fate and chance will even out in the end. We tie our hope to man's progress—the advances of science, technology, and medicine. If we search long enough, we can explain the unexplained. Scholars and PhD's posit theories from evolution to karma and provide logical constructs to deal with the mysteries of our universe.

We are comfortable with this scientific approach yet perturbed by its repercussions. We revere Darwin's survival of the fittest theory yet are shocked by violence and war. We laud the efficiency of markets yet famine and pestilence affront us. We say truth is relative and tolerance is king yet we are outraged by injustice.

As devotees of the Alpha Man Code, we take the rational path by trusting Self before trusting God. Is the supernatural too ethereal and esoteric or just unfamiliar? If we don't believe in God, why? What is our *specific* rationale? The question is too important for each of us not to have a cogent and well-conceived position.

---

## One Man's Story

*Stephen lived with a hastily constructed worldview. He grew up in a prominent Jewish family in Philadelphia. They were a close-knit flock of Eagles fans, active in their community and synagogue. After college, Stephen moved to New York to pursue a career in sales.*

*Stephen was an intense leader who rose to senior vice president of an internet media company. He pressed his team to put everything into their work. At the end of each quarter, Stephen became grouchy, rude, and anxious about hitting the projected numbers. As a result, he was respected more than liked by staff members.*

*Stephen was committed to raising his children according to Jewish tradition. When his oldest daughter turned four, Stephen realized he needed a better understanding of Judaism.*

*He queried family members about Jewish holidays and festivals. Though he had fond memories from his youth, it struck Stephen that he had never explored God's place in these celebrations. How could he consider himself "religious" without seriously contemplating God?*

*"Who is Jesus?" his daughter asked after school one day. Stephen didn't know. Questions flooded his mind:*

Is God real? Did He create the Heavens and Earth? Did His Son live in this world? Is Jesus the Messiah?

*Stephen was surprised how much his uncertainty about these foundational questions affected him. He felt lost at home. He struggled at work. Without a clear understanding of what he believed and why he believed it, Stephen could not lead or inspire others effectively.*

Many of us are like Stephen. Our perspective on Self is clear but our view on God is sketchy. Bad experiences with religion or lack of interest keep us from exploring a critically important issue for us and our families. Knowing what we believe about God is essential to understanding ourselves.

## Do I Count?

In the epic film *Troy,*[13] based on Homer's poem *The Iliad,* the ruthless Greek warrior Achilles leads his band of men against the Trojans. The odds against them are overwhelming. Death is almost certain. As their small boat approaches the shore of the fortified enemy city Achilles turns to his men and shouts, "Beyond that beach…is immortality!" The men roar at this chance to become legend.

Alpha men's intense desire to make a name for our self is reiterated in the film's final line when the narrator states, "Let them say I lived in the time of Achilles."

Why are we so desperate to be remembered? Listening to men boast about their goal-obsessed, calendar-choking, technology-laden, be-on-the-cutting-edge lives, I often wonder, *What are we trying to prove?*

Our ego is a contributor to this bloated machismo. What is the ego? How does it work?

According to Freud, the ego serves as a governor switch, balancing our primitive drives (gratification of biological needs) with our conscience (morals and understanding of right and wrong). A healthy ego reins in our lusts and appetites. Conversely, a dysfunctional ego allows primal impulses to go unchecked. This leads to indulgence and an attitude of entitlement. Instinctual drivers like aggressiveness and desire takeover.

Self-centered alpha men like myself have big—dysfunctional—egos. (That's why Me, Inc. was hatched.) The ego serves as a barometer for our sense of self. It is easily intoxicated by success, riding high with our achievements. String together a couple of wins and our ego becomes Mr. Ego.

An overinflated view of one's self is like Mr. Ego on steroids. Excessive pride comes from an bloated self-appraisal. Conceit, envy, and jealousy are Mr. Ego's characteristics.

We recognize the arrogance of Mr. Ego in other guys, but seldom in ourselves. Understanding the make-up of Mr. Ego is essential to addressing his dominion. Let's break down an unhealthy ego's three flaws:

**Mr. Ego is comparative**. "The ego gets no pleasure out of having something, only having more of it than the next person,"[14] wrote C.S. Lewis, author of *The Chronicles of Narnia* and many other renowned works. Lewis suggests our ego operates through distinction and differentiation. Everything is relative, our accomplishments are meaningful only if they are better than the next guy's. This phenomenon explains the Amplified Reference Anxiety plague. For example, the joy I felt earning my biggest bonus was ruined by learning others received more.

**Mr. Ego is immature**. We *have* to be better than others. Ego builds itself up by bringing others down. Like a boyhood bully, Mr. Ego picks on the puniest kid in the schoolyard. This is why alpha men compare our strengths against others' weaknesses.

**Mr. Ego is insatiable.** Despite all of our achievements, our egos always crave more. Seeking acceptance and respect, affirmation and adulation, feeding Mr. Ego is a never-ending endeavor. It requires a steady stream of public adulation and respect.

To test the condition of your ego, insert key drivers in your life between the brackets below:

- Hang in there, honey, as soon as I [*make partner/close this big deal*], I'll spend more time with you and the kids
- If I just [*get a song published/open my own practice*], I will feel like I have arrived.
- [*Finishing this triathlon/My son's athletic scholarship*] will show everyone what I'm made of.
- I'm only going to [*get high/sleep with my assistant*] this one last time.

If any of these statements ring true then perhaps you are trying to prove something to somebody. How will you quell Mr. Ego? Who answers "Do I count?" for you? Your dad? Your buddies? Your wife? Will the revolving door of women affirm your virility? If they say you are awesome today, will you still feel fulfilled tomorrow? What if they change their mind? How long will you be a slave to their opinion?

**Our masculinity is bestowed not acquired.** While we can act "manly," we cannot confirm manhood upon ourselves. Donning a pastel cardigan and announcing to our reflection, *"I'm good enough, I'm smart enough and doggone it, people like me,"*[15] is an effective affirmation for Stuart Smalley but not in real life.

Who determines a man's worthiness? How do we know if we count? The apostle Paul wrote, **"It is the Lord who judges me."**[16] God is our final arbitrator. He is the ultimate authority.

This is a controversial perspective and hard to swallow. If after all your accomplishments and successes you are still trying to prove yourself then consider the possibility that God will be the one to answer your query "Do I count?"

## Where do I stand?

Submitting ourselves to God's judgment is unnerving. What criteria does He use to assess us? How do we measure up? Are we doomed by all the transgressions we committed over our lifetime?

You know when a coach grabs you by both shoulders to get your attention or the boss calls you in his office and asks you to shut the door? The next thing out of their mouth is going to be important.

Don't miss this!

Based on personal experience and discussions with other alpha men, I've concluded the root of men's discontent and the source of our inner turmoil comes from a single unanswered question. **The source of men's emptiness, fear, isolation, anger, resentment, addiction, even depression is our inability to resolve our question "Where do I stand with God?"**

You can disagree with me, you can be outraged, or you can write me off as biased. But do not ignore this question. Whether you believe in God or not, whether you actively pursue a relationship with Him or actively avoid Him, at least test this assertion thoroughly.

Millions of men's lives have been transformed because they took the time to explore their standing with God. Some were followers of God and others didn't know Him. Some were worldly successes and others barely subsisted. However, they all recognized their cultural prescription for happiness and success was incomplete and their internal conflict was real.

There is an alternative to the Alpha Man Code paradigm that explains the emotional and spiritual firestorm inside of us.

I didn't know God was the answer nor was I seeking Him. **God found me.** When I was in my darkest moments, God reached out a hand to help. He cared for me. Once I realized where I stood with him, my life changed. I am part of God's family. I *do* count. I am worthy. God is with me.

Throughout the rest of the book, we'll examine how a relationship with God dramatically affects our lives.

# FIVE

# A New Man Code

## Reformation of Man

Men are better than our actions demonstrate. We possess unbridled potential. Let's stop settling for mediocrity and strive for a more meaningful impact on our corner of the world.

I believe a new vision can dawn for every guy: the Reformation of Man. We will be honorable men who stand by our values and convictions. Integrity will be our hallmark, trustworthiness our distinction. We will fulfill obligations and be accountable for actions at home as well as at work.

We will be better stewards, generous with our time and money. **Men will determine wealth by what *we give away*, rather than what we stockpile.** We can be rich in good deeds and legendary for our sharing and sacrifice. We will define our identity by the core values for which we stand.

Men will remove our Alpha Man Code masks and tear down the walls around our hearts. We will stop hiding and pretending. Transparency will come naturally.

Our new vision of manhood rejects inflated egos and exposes the perils of pride. Self no longer needs to be our deity. Breaking this allegiance enables men to lead by honesty, humility, and self-control.

Hope will be based on God's promises and provision. Faith will be placed in His plan for us rather than our expertise, competency or guile. Significance will come from serving God rather than indulging ourselves.

If you want to stand out from the crowd, stand up against Self. If you want to be a revolutionary, be the first to focus on "who I am" rather than "who I know" or "what I do." If you feel rebellious, ditch the designer labels, tattoos, profanity, and all the external junk you use to prove your manhood. If you want to start a movement, surrender to personal accountability.

Gentlemen, influencers impact the world and men of character are influencers.


# Men of Impact

John Wooden made an impact. The legendary UCLA basketball coach won ten NCAA championships, including seven in a row, and a record four undefeated seasons. A generation of coaches and a lineage of NBA all-stars are proof of his significance to college basketball.

During his tenure at UCLA, Wooden did not actively recruit players to be part of his championship squads. And surprisingly, he never spoke about winning with his team or coaches. Contrasted with today's win-at-all-costs sports culture, his style seems flawed. How did he achieve such exceptional success? How can his approach help us?

Coach Wooden sought men of character, not just top athletes. The best way to attract these players was to model the traits he desired from them.

As a high school senior, Lew Alcindor was the most highly-recruited player in the country. Alcindor (Kareem Adul-Jabbar) led UCLA to three NCAA championships and eighty-eight victories in ninety games. Yet Wooden never initiated a call to Alcindor or his family to sell him on UCLA. How did Alcindor end up with the Bruins?

"[Coach Wooden] built his basketball program a certain way—athletically, ethically, morally—because he believed it would attract a certain type of person," Alcindor recalled. "I chose UCLA in large part because what I saw and heard about those values."[17] What John Wooden stood for was so attractive that the nation's top center inquired about how to become part of his team. That's influence.

In Bennis and Nanus' best-seller on leadership they state, "The essential factor in leadership is the ability to influence."[18] Alpha men are natural commanders but not always effective leaders. We can order people around but can we connect to them on an intrinsic level.

What is the secret to capturing hearts and gaining loyalty? How do we become influencers?

Influence comes in two flavors:

- Positional—when one's role gives them authority over another.
- Personal—when one leads without the benefit of a title or post.

Positional influence is tied to power. Many find this style of leadership effective, yet it can be fraught with the temptation for abuse. Leaders who rely on positional influence often manipulate, exploit, or rule by fear. Leveraging the power of a title, one can influence others to compromise standards against their judgment.

The familiar saying "Power corrupts, absolute power corrupts absolutely" remains relevant. We all have horror stories about a tyrant boss who ruled by harsh tactics we did not respect or emulate. In family situations, we can exploit physical or emotional power to appease selfish motives. Men who rely on their position or prowess to lead are giants on the outside but midgets on the inside.

Positional influence is only temporary. Allegiance is provisional. Followers will comply out of duty or obligation, jumping ship as soon as something better comes along. Eventually, power dissipates and leaders fade away.

**Personal influence is generated by core values, convictions and conduct.** The source of personal influence is the depth of one's heart, not the sharpness of one's mind or the breadth of one's network. It is about investing in others rather than intimidating them. Serving others first creates a strong connection between a leader and his followers: loyalty based on respect and authenticity.

One of the most influential men of all time was Jesus of Nazareth. Jesus had only two positions on his resume—carpenter and Son of God. Dr. Martin Luther King noted that Jesus never wrote a book, held an office, had a family, owned a house, went to college, or visited a big city.

Though he did none of the things the world associates with greatness, Dr. King said Jesus "stands as the most influential figure that ever entered human history. All of the armies that ever marched, all the navies that ever sailed, all the parliaments that ever sat, and all the kings that ever reigned put together have not affected the life of man on this earth as much as that one solitary life."[19]

The relationship between Jesus and God established the strength of character and the depth of his heart to be so profoundly influential.

## Forging Character

Warren Bennis wrote, "Successful leadership is not about being tough or soft, sensitive or assertive, but about a set of attributes. First and foremost is character."

Character has been pondered for ages, from the ancient Greeks to current geeks. The word is derived from the Greek term *charaktêr*, a mark stamped on a coin or a seal pressed into wax. Socrates, Plato, and Aristotle linked character to virtue or moral excellence, an ideal one sought to attain. This classical view of character emphasizes the exercise of reason. Virtue and vice are evaluated within the context of what was good or right. Humility, integrity, and self-control are essential components of character.

Dr. King awoke our nation when he dreamed of a day when we would not be judged by the color of our skin but the content of our character. Unfortunately, many of us undervalue our character.

The Alpha Man Code reinforces the temptation to compromise. We don't stick to internal values but shift according to our surroundings. Ethics are situational. Morals are circumstantial. Sadly, we assuage any guilt from bending the rules by redesigning right and wrong to meet our needs. In this way, any action we take can be justified.

The corruption of character takes its toll: trust is broken, people lose faith in one another, personal agendas feed skepticism, and lack of authenticity brings out the cynic in all of us. Billy Graham said, "When wealth is lost, nothing is lost. When health is lost, something is lost; when character is lost, all is lost."

At one point in my career, my character seemed lost. I was so obsessed with goals and timeframes to succeed I cut corners to keep my momentum. Whenever we put winning above everything else, we will do almost anything to win. Eventually, my short-sighted strategy failed. As challenges mounted, I struggled. With a weak character during tough times, I could not lead my work life or personal life effectively.

Coach Wooden defines competitive greatness as **"being at your best when your best is needed."** Character is poise under pressure; our consistency and calm in the midst of conflict. This is the personal resource I desire most. I want to be a man others count on in the clutch. Strengthening character is an ongoing battle.

**Character is forged not found.** It is tested by both prosperity and adversity. Hundreds of small decisions we make in the heat of daily battle hone our character. These challenges either strengthen us or wear us down.

Nobel laureate Nelson Mandela offers insight on character development. Commenting on his comrades who fought racial injustice in South Africa he said, "The decades of oppression and brutality had another unintended effect, producing men of such extraordinary courage, wisdom and generosity that their like may never be known again. Perhaps it requires such depth of oppression to create such heights of character."

We all have notions of what is right or good: some of us convert those thoughts into actions; others do not. Why do men like Mandela overcome hardship while others buckle?

## One Man's Story

*Tony Dungy, head coach of the Super Bowl champion Indianapolis Colts, understands the importance of character during swings of prosperity and adversity.*

*In the 1970s, Coach Dungy faced the NFL establishment's prejudice against black quarterbacks. Whispers about race and intelligence haunted him as he tried to secure head coaching positions over the next two decades. He proved skeptics wrong by leading both the Tampa Bay Bucs and the Colts to the playoffs.*

*Then Coach Dungy faced a terrible tragedy: his teenage son committed suicide. It is impossible to fathom the anguish any parent experiences when they lose a child. Coach Dungy's relationship with God strengthened his character and provided the resolve to pull him through his grief.*

***Crisis reveals our character.*** *While many men would have collapsed, Coach Dungy took his coaching to another level. He led the Colts to a Super Bowl victory within 18 months of his son's death!*

*How can any man lead so well under such dire circumstances?*

*Coach Dungy's leadership style was not founded in the Alpha Man Code. His integrity and level of authenticity was a sharp contrast to traditional NFL coaching and Alpha Man practices. He never cursed nor raised his voice. He treated his players with respect and built a high level of trust. He was authentic about his feelings and fears. He even prayed with them. And he gave God the credit for the championship.*

*Many of his peers want to be legendary coaches measured by wins and championships. Coach Dungy's legend will center on his character and influence. "Winning the Super Bowl was a goal I've had for a long time. But it has never been my purpose in life," Dungy wrote in his autobiography,* Quiet Strength. *"I coach football. But the good I can do to glorify God along the way is my real purpose."*

I believe Coach Dungy's Super Bowl victory is a seminal moment in the reformation of man. **He epitomizes a new leadership culture where character and integrity developed through a relationship with God are valued as much as competence and the bottom line.** If this leadership style works in a gladiator sport like football, it can help all of our workplaces and communities.

Building character is a journey we take with God. God has a part and we have a part.

"Rejoice in our suffering," the Apostle Paul wrote in his letter to the Romans. Come again?! "Because we know that **suffering produces perseverance, perseverance character and character, hope.** And hope does not disappoint us because God has poured out his love into our hearts by the Holy Spirit."[20]

Though it sounds inhumane that our relationship with God grows through suffering, in fact, it is not human—it's holy.

Tribulation is a test to see who we will trust: Self or God. When we suffer, we can try making it on our own or turn to Him. Challenges we face are opportunities to strengthen our heart and fortify our commitment to rely on God first.

Understanding God's role in developing character is essential for me. His active engagement in my life gives me new perspective on the trials I face. Adversity is not random happenstance, but rather a vital aspect of God's larger plan to bless me my life. Like Tony Dungy, I rely on God and live by a New Man Code.

## A Radical Paradigm

For many alpha men, the current Man Code has lost its significance. We want a standard to inspire us and stimulate our growth. Men are seeking an approach that creates radical change, not marginal improvement.

Bucking long-held dogma like the Alpha Man Code is challenging. Wars have erupted for less. Such dramatic change requires men brave enough to contest cultural norms.

If "Every Man for Himself" epitomizes the Alpha Man Code, then let **"Leave No Man Behind"** capture the spirit of a New Man Code. Here is my proposal:

**A New Man Code**

- Trust God and Trust Others
- Character is the New Currency
- Be a Strong-Hearted Man
- Define Identity Through Our Relationship with God
- Demonstrate Relational Excellence and Personal Equity
- Be Authentic, Accepting, and Available
- Serve Others Rather than Solve Others
- Invest in One Another
- Leave No Man Behind

This radical doctrine is transformational. It starts when we cede authority to God. Serving one another trumps serving Self. We will minister to the physical, emotional and spiritual needs of others. Courage and humility will emanate from a strong heart, not an iron will.

Relational excellence provides richer connections with our family, our buddies, and work colleagues. We will focus on what we can give rather than what we can get. Developing our character, trustworthiness, and authenticity will help us commit to God and one another.

Moving these New Man Code components off the page and into our lives is a challenging. We can't do it on our own; help from other guys is essential. Living a New Man Code is best experienced in the bonds of fellowship.

Gentlemen, we are each at a crossroads. We have the opportunity to change our life dramatically. We understand the pitfalls of a self-directed, alpha man lifestyle. Regardless of where we stand on God, at least we should consider the alternative vision for a journey with God in command.

Abiding by the tenets of the New Man Code each of us can become the men we were destined to be. Not only can we finish strong, we can make an impact.

Alpha men want to change the world. First, we have to change ourselves.

# SIX

# Change From the Inside Out

## Can Men Change?

In the small Texas town of Gruene a message on the water tower reads, "Gently resisting change since 1872."

Alpha men do not defy change very gently. Renowned for our innovation and entrepreneurial spirit, we can also be rigid and regimented. We resist the necessary steps to examine flaws and modify our ways.

Inertia is one of our biggest stumbling-blocks. Only when crisis threatens us do men concede the status quo. At first, we try to get by with only minor behavioral modifications. These surface alterations rarely address misguided motivations or attitudes and thus have nominal long-term impact.

Personally, I hate change. As a creature of habit, once I get into a routine, I wear it out.

I walk thirty blocks to and from work. There are a zillion possible paths along Manhattan streets to get there. Occasionally, my wife stops by the office with our sons and we walk home as a family. Everything is cool until we hit a street light. Once, at a corner where I normally continue north my wife crossed the street and headed east.

"Where are you going?" I demanded in a tone fit for a straying dog.

57

"We're going home."

"That's the wrong way."

"It's not the *wrong* way," she called from halfway to the other corner, "it's just not *your* way."

Then the boys witnessed their lunatic father make an impassioned speech as to why his way is the *only* way. When I realized the silliness of my argument, I brooded all the way home.

That never happens to you though, right? You are *wide* open to change.

---

## One Man's Story

*Matt is a singer/songwriter with a new CD and a promising future. His struggle with change threatened his music career and his marriage.*

*Growing up in rural Oklahoma, Matt learned to respect his elders and follow the Golden Rule. He complied with church-centered culture until he ran across a Playboy magazine and decided, "I need to get me one of them girls."*

*Matt picked up guitar and pursued the life of a rock star. Though he gained a college scholarship to sing opera, his passion was heavy metal. His garage band became a local legend, playing frat houses and bars throughout the Southwest. They were featured on the radio and sang for thousands as an opening act for nationally renowned groups. His college days became a round-the-clock high on sex, alcohol, and weed.*

*Matt met Megan when the two starred in the rock opera Tommy. She was the gorgeous pin-up he always wanted and the first for whom Matt sacrificed his throngs of disposable girls. The two seemed like the perfect couple.*

*Matt wanted to write music "to touch peoples' hearts" but was so fogged by drugs he didn't know his own heart. Frustration with his stalled creativity spilled into his relationship with Megan. The two fought incessantly, always on the verge of a break-up.*

*Megan threatened to leave unless Matt cleaned up his act. First, he promised to kick his drug habit. Matt even convinced Megan to get married. Things were better for a while, but sadly, Matt's changes didn't last.*

*The couple moved to New York to take on a bigger stage. Megan's career blossomed and she toured with Broadway shows. Matt stumbled. The underground music scene was crowded, and nobody cared that he was a big dog in Oklahoma.*

*Then, Matt was busted buying drugs on the street. New York City narcs gave him the strip-squat-and-cough routine before throwing him in jail. He couldn't connect with Megan for days. Their marriage barely survived the black out.*

*To cover the bills, Matt took a job as a butler at an investment bank. He served executives coffee and scones. Lonely without Megan for months at a time, Matt blew their cash on pot. His writing flailed and he got high all day sulking in their dumpy apartment.*

Matt didn't anticipate the twists and turns his life took. To resurrect his music career and provide a future for his family, Matt had to make major changes. Unfortunately, modifications of his behavior did not alter who he was on the inside.

Real change requires a transformation—we have to become new men, not just the same guy with patches covering our rough spots and holes.

## Change by Crisis Only

Over coffee and bad airport food, a colleague of mine told me, "A man's fate is sealed by the time he is twelve." In my buddy's view, our temperament and personality are formed in concrete during youth. There is little one can do to alter the outcome. Our lot is our lot, period, end of story.

I find this fatalistic viewpoint sad. While I congratulate those men whose lives are following the right blueprint, what about the rest of us? If the trajectory of our life is off, are we doomed?

Men must first acknowledge change is possible. Next, we have to see our need for change. That is the big hurdle.

A talented writer and friend Chris Burge teaches, **"Men change due to crisis.** Modifications come out of desperation rather than revelation."[21]

For most alpha men, personal change is a defensive reaction rather than an offensive strategy. We wait for situations to force our hand instead of usinilable information to initiate change. If we ran a business this poorly we wouldn't be in charge long. Men hang onto old routines and habits, waiting for different outcomes. It's like the old quip, "The definition of insanity is doing the same thing over and over and expecting different results." Smoking kills us yet we can't kick the habit; cholesterol clogs our arteries but we still Super Size our fries; abusing alcohol and drugs pulls us down but we keep going back; pornography and gambling destroy families yet we continue to partake.

"When we are no longer able to change a situation," noted Victor Frankl, "we are challenged to change ourselves."[22] Much of men's cynicism and resentment is rooted in our inability to modify our own behavior.

Change is essential to growth. Growth is essential to life.

Below are some indicators that can help determine what change is necessary in our lives. Getting a buddy to give you an objective perspective on these areas is very helpful.

1. **External signals:** Do you feel your leadership at work has peaked? Are you indifferent or dissatisfied with your marriage? Are you estranged from your kids? Do addictions control you?
2. **Internal signals:** Do you feel empty or unfulfilled? Do you lack a vision for your future? Are you paralyzed by fear or insecurity? Do you struggle with your identity—a true understanding of who you are? Have you lost hope?
3. **Spiritual signals:** Are you unsure about God and His role in your life? Do you worry about where you stand with Him? Do you wish to build your relationship with God?

Hopefully, these questions will help you assess your need for change. If so, how do we create lasting change?

## Modification vs. Transformation

There are many popular means to enact change. Diet plans, twelve-step programs, gum, pills, shots, and mind tricks all promise to alter our appetites and quell bad habits. These behavioral modification techniques employ external stimuli to impact actions and behaviors—change from the outside in. In addition to self-help marketers, corporations spend big bucks on behavioral modification methods to upgrade management skills and ensure compliance with business directives.

While behavioral modification goes by many spiffy monikers, it is mostly a rehash of the venerable carrot and stick. If you put enough wealth, power, and status in one corner, people will chase them; if you supply fear, shame, or guilt in the other corner people will avoid them.

**Behavioral modification lasts only as long as a stimulus is in place.** Remove the incentive or the deterrent and individuals will fall back to their old ways.

It's like a hot shot showing up at the first tee sporting his $1000 driver with a plutonium shaft and a head the size of a holiday ham. While bragging about the club's astrophysical properties, he takes a few practice swings. Everyone realizes replacing his old driver will only change how far he hits his ball into the woods or how deep into the lake.

A new club will not fix a bad swing. Should we expect the latest behavioral techniques to be more effective than the latest golf technology?

Change from the inside out is radically different approach with appreciably better results. Here's a familiar example.

At the beginning of Charles Dickens' *A Christmas Carol,* the miserly Scrooge is described as "Hard and sharp as flint, from which no steel had ever struck out a generous fire, secret, and self-contained, and solitary as an oyster." He is an efficient and rational man. Scrooge is not susceptible to petty emotions like compassion or empathy. His cold-heartedness is displayed as a pair of businessmen solicited him:

"I don't make merry myself at Christmas," said Scrooge, "and I can't afford to make the people merry. I help to support establishments I have mentioned [prisons and workhouses]— they cost enough: and those who are badly off must go there."

One man replied, "Many can't go there; and many would rather die."

"If they would rather die," said Scrooge, "they better do it, and decrease the surplus population." This was one bitter man uninterested in changing his ways.

Overnight, Scrooge had an intense spiritual encounter with three ghosts. He arose with a fresh perspective.

After sending a boy off to Bob Cratchit's house with the largest goose in London, Scrooge exhibited his new demeanor: "The chuckle with which [Scrooge] said this and the chuckle with which he paid for the goose, and the chuckle with which he paid for the cab, and the chuckle with which he recompensed the boy, were only to be exceeded by the chuckle with which he sat down breathless again and chuckled till he cried."

No one paid or threatened Scrooge to act charitably. His whole demeanor and character transformed from a hard-as-flint ogre to a chuckling friend and generous boss. Scrooge transformed from the inside out and became a new man.

The difference between behavioral modification and personal transformation is profound. One is incremental and the other is revolutionary. One is an enhancement to our lifestyle while the other is a radical rebirth. One is safe and the other risky. One is routine and the other is adventuresome. One is controllable and the other is explosive. One is a learned technique and the other is a supernatural wonder.

**Behavioral modification is barely noticeable to anyone. Personal transformation is unmistakable to everyone.**

Matt experienced transformation that started within and worked through all facets of his life. He kicked his drug addiction and his marriage is blooming. With a clear head and a clean heart, his song writing is prolific. His words and music illuminate the suffering as well as the hope and redemption he experienced.

Matt is a new man and he loves to sing about it.

## The Power of Transformation

Personal transformation can change a man and alter history. Consider the impact of the apostle Paul and the Christian church on the fate of the Roman Empire.[23]

Born as Saul of Tarsus (his Hebrew name), Paul was a member of the Jewish elite class, the Pharisees. An intellectually and culturally astute man, he attended university and was well versed in Greek language, poetry and debate. He even attained Roman citizenship.

Saul despised the "Followers of the Way," those claiming Jesus as the Christ (Messiah). Saul became a notorious oppressor of early Christians. In a letter recounting his earlier days, he wrote, "I violently persecuted God's church. I did my best to destroy it."

Luke, author of the Bible's book of Acts,[24] described the experience that changed Saul's life. A doctor by trade, Luke was an exacting reporter. He meticulously detailed this encounter that took place well after the crucifixion between Saul and the resurrected Jesus.

"When traveling to Damascus, as Saul and his two colleagues were walking, he was struck down by a brilliant light.

"'Saul, Saul why do you persecute me?'

"'Who are you, Lord?' Saul asked.

"'I am Jesus, whom you are persecuting,' He replied. 'Now get up and go into the city and you will be told what to do.'"

Those traveling with Saul were speechless. They heard a sound but saw nothing. Saul was blinded and was led by hand into Damascus.

Three days later, in the house of a friend on Straight Street (which still exists), Jesus communicated to Saul that he was to be "my chosen instrument to carry my name before Gentiles and their kings and before the people of Israel." Saul's sight was then miraculously restored.

Immediately, Saul began preaching in the local synagogues that Jesus was, in fact, the Son of God. The Jews were astonished! How could such a fervent tormentor of Jesus' followers claim He was the Messiah? This was preposterous! This was unbelievable!

Saul, who later took his Roman name Paul, became a leader of the Christian movement. He never wavered on the details of his Damascus Road encounter with Christ that transformed him from a persecutor to a pursuer of Jesus.

Paul's personal testimony led to an explosion of the Christian faith across the Middle East and Mediterranean region. He penned much of the Bible's New Testament, including thirteen letters to blossoming congregations in Rome, Corinth, Ephesus, Philippi and other major cities. As the early Christian movement exploded the power and authority of the Roman Empire waned.

64

When you consider the millions of lives changed by Paul's writings, his personal transformation is one of the most influential in history.

I heard stories of men being reborn. I witnessed guys go through radical change in their lives. These testimonies gave me hope. I could relate to their circumstances. I understood the emotions they were feeling because I had been there myself. I was encouraged that real change was possible for me as well.

Are you ready for real change? Perhaps your life has fallen into a routine like Phil Connors' (Bill Murray) in *Groundhog Day*. Phil was stuck in Punxsutawney, PA, waking up morning after morning at 5:59 AM to a sappy Sonny and Cher song on his clock radio. Phil wrecked his car, got shot, stabbed, drowned, poisoned, electrocuted, asphyxiated—*anything* to escape a life of endless repetition.

If you are trapped in a similar nightmare, consider embarking on real change. Transformation from the inside out is radical, and difficult, and your life will never be the same.

SEVEN

# Strong-Hearted Men

## Start at the Core

Transformation at our core sounds intriguing. So what's the drill? Do we discipline ourselves better? Can we execute a five-step process, employ a meditation technique, or swallow new blue pill?

The theologian St. Augustine (354-430 AD) wrote, "The key to life change is not the act of the will but in the loves of the heart."

Is this guy serious? An alpha men's willpower is certainly strong enough to create substantive change. It's obvious that St. Augustine hasn't been watching *The Sopranos*. That show demonstrates men have very tough wills. And Bada Bing, lives *are* changing.

Our performance culture values intelligence and competence. The mind is the means of getting to the top of the corporate, community or political realm. The Alpha Man Code instructs us to ignore our heart or covers it up. Yet many men following this cold, mechanical approach experience shallow, empty lives.

Could Augustine be right? Is the heart the source of change?

Truth is, alpha men know little about our heart.

Physically, the heart is a vital organ. It is chock-full of aortas, ventricles and other high-school biology terms we can't remember until our first bypass. The heart is our internal power plant, pumping energy through our body, day after day, year after year. It is the muscle of vitality and passion driving us forward.

The heart is also the canvas of love, capable of extraordinary joy and excruciating pain. Relationships are the music of our heart and intimacy the dance. The nature of love is a perplexing, yet we all fall under its spell. One minute, we soar like an eagle and the next we wallow like a boar. Our heart's fragile nature makes us feel incompetent and impotent.

A favorite scene of mine from the movie *Jaws*[25] unveils this dichotomy. Drunk on homemade hooch, Quint, Matt Hooper, and Chief Brody huddled in the *Orca's* cabin late one night comparing seafaring scars.

Hooper hauled up the leg of his jeans and boasted, "Bull shark scraped me while I was taking samples."

"Nothing!" snarled the old salt Quint. He drained his shot glass, revealed a scar on his calf and growled, "Look here— slammed by a thresher's tail."

They laughed, drank to their legs, and compared other wounds.

Then, Hooper declared the topper of all toppers. He pulled open his shirt: "Right there," Hooper said, jabbing at his chest. The others looked blankly. "Mary Ellen Moffit…she broke my heart."

Hooper roared and so do I every time I watch this scene. But to a man suffering from a broken heart, it's no laughing matter. The pain is unbearable.

The notion of a broken heart exists in every culture and every era. From ancient Chinese poetry to Shakespeare to post-modern novels, this affliction fascinates us. No one knows a complete cure and workings of the heart remain a mystery.

To experience conversion at our core, we must better understand the complex make-up of our heart and its maladies.

## Heart is the Source

I had a heart deficit. This gap was a major impediment to my personal and professional growth. Due in part to fear and in part to ignorance, I chose not to deal with the problem.

History shows the best leaders are not always the smartest or most persuasive. **Intelligence and charisma can take us to places our heart can't sustain.** This was a painful lesson for me. My heart deficit first affected me at work, putting the brakes on my professional climb.

Risk taking was a cornerstone of my early career. Traditional paths took too long. I zeroed in on new product launches and turnarounds, gateways to success or the corporate graveyard. Within ten years, I achieved my goal of General Manager. My future seemed limitless.

As I rose higher at my firm, I faced increasingly difficult challenges. Decisions became choices between right and right or wrong and wrong. There was little black and white, only gray. The complexity of leading leaders rather than managing managers staggered me. My title gained compliance, but it couldn't garner confidence. At this level, I needed wisdom, not robotic management techniques.

I looked the part of the senior executive, performing procedures and processes in the "right" manner. Under the surface, my motivations and attitudes were a mess. Without a clear understanding of my core values and convictions, I waffled. I did not have the inner strength to influence such experienced executives.

In his book *Integrity* leading corporate consultant Dr. Henry Cloud wrote, "The human heart will seek to be known, understood, and connected with above all else. If you do not connect, the ones you care about will find someone who will."[26]

I understood the concept of building this type of intrinsic bond with others but, frankly, I was a relational greenhorn. Changing my style of leadership to connect more deeply with my staff was daunting and scary.

Take for instance my open door policy. People walked in and I let them vent. I didn't bother listening. Instead, my brain buzzed with strategies to fix their problem. I focused on neutralizing conflict and calming waters. Though I acted interested, I didn't address the origins of my coworkers' dilemmas or the impact on them personally.

Lacking empathy, my words were patronizing and arrogant. This served to invalidate the emotions of people I was meant to lead—and alienate them forever. Let me repeat, alienate them forever!

Soon, staff members stopped walking in the door. I became a leader without followers.

**A heart deficit created a glass ceiling in my career.** Years of education and experience could not overcome an immature heart. I was no better at home. Relationally, I cultivated minimal intimacy with little promise of improvement. I didn't understand the root causes of my relational mediocrity, nor did I apply extra effort.

My future seemed bleak. Work had topped out, my marriage was bottoming out, and I felt powerless to enact change.

I lost hope.

## Finding Hope

For our heart to remain healthy, **men need hope.**

What is hope? I hope I close this deal? I hope the Giants win the Super Bowl? I hope I can pay for my kids' education?

Webster's defines hope as, "a wish or desire accomplished with expectation of fulfillment." Therefore, **hope is a certainty, a strong belief in a future outcome.** Hope isn't just an expression of what would make our lives more comfortable, it's a desire we expect to fulfill. We can't wish to save enough for retirement or desire our marriage to last—we must place our trust and efforts somewhere that perpetuates hope no matter what happens.

Maybe our hope is not in the right place. If we build our hope in our career, marriage, bank account, or son's athletic career, we set ourselves up for devastation. If the object of our hope crashes and burns, so will we.

Hope based on our capabilities or resourcefulness makes us slaves to our desires. With lives centered on achievement, we are shackled to our careers. If we thrive on human approval, we are serfs to opinion. When those things fail us, hope can evaporate.

Without hope, men are dead in the water.

What does real hope feel like?

I've been a lifelong Red Sox fan. It was a miserable existence, until 2004! After the Sox fell behind three games to none in the 2004 pennant series against the Yankees, I did not watch the end of game four. (Shameful, I know.) During the most exciting, exhilarating comeback in Red Sox history, I went to bed early.

Years of disappointment left me with no hope. Even after the Sox pulled out a win in game four, watching games five, six, and seven was torture. Because the outcome of each game was uncertain, I worried so much about the final score that I took no pleasure in the back and forth of each inning. The victory was satisfying but I never enjoyed the adventure of the game in progress.

Hope can change our perspective entirely.

Suppose a reliable source revealed to me that the Red Sox would win the 2004 pennant race. He didn't disclose how or when, only that, in the end, the Sox would win be American League champs. Imagine how much better my experience would have been! My demeanor would have been brighter. I would have celebrated the swings in momentum in each game rather than agonized through them because of my expectation for the Red Sox to triumph.

What if our lives could be like this? What if we start every morning expecting to prevail?

Think how different each day would be if we were *certain* that, regardless of ups and downs and the brutality of the daily fist-fight, we would be fine. With this hope, we could enjoy the adventure of life. **We could celebrate our present condition because we would have reason to hope and expect the outcome of our ultimate future.**

Remember Doug? He was desperate for hope. He wanted assurance that his life would change. Fixing his circumstances would not cut it. Making up with his wife and getting his family back would help but these situational changes would not be a source of hope. Doug needed something larger than himself, more potent than his own willpower. He needed to derive hope in something eternal.

## The Eternal Stamp

A friend once told me that real hope comes from a belief in eternal life. I had to chew on this declaration. Eternity is a difficult notion. It's hard to wrap our minds around an infinite existence. Fortunately, we don't have to. The concept is ingrained in us.

The Bible states, "God has set eternity in the hearts of men."[27] God brands each of us with a transcendent fingerprint. Whether we choose to believe in Him or not, God's mark is etched on our hearts.

Why do alpha men quiver at the thought of being inconsequential? Like Achilles attacking Troy, we yearn for immortality. **Men crave something permanent in a life we acknowledge as temporary.** Whether in business, art, music, sports, or whatever, we are desperate to leave an everlasting imprint.

Long before I wrangled with the question of God, I lusted for an enduring legacy. My childhood fantasies were heroic efforts of winning the big game or taking a bullet for someone else. While the details changed over the years, my dreams of immortality continued.

If eternity is our destination, then we are certain we will prevail. This is real hope, hope which replaces emptiness, fear and isolation with peace. **Hope founded in God's promises rather than our own performance provides the fortitude to overcome struggles and suffering.**

A biblical proverb says, "Guard your heart, for it is the well-spring of life."[28] Our heart produces our deepest passions. It shapes our motivations and attitudes. Our heart communicates between our brain and our soul.

Battlefield heroism and courageous athletic performances are often attributed to the heart rather than skill or savvy. We describe individuals prevailing despite wounds, injuries, or overwhelming odds as having the "heart of a lion." The heart—not the head—is the source of bravery and sacrifice on the behalf of others. Such spectacular selflessness is less about reason and more about inner strength to overcome fear. That is how we become strong-hearted men.

For me God's fingerprint on my heart changes everything. I can see a bigger picture for my life, a long-term perspective that provides wisdom for handling short-term challenges. I am better prepared to persevere when facing volatile circumstances. My work is not limited to what I accomplish at the office. My relationships grow and sustain me, rather than deplete me. With the New Man Code as my guide, I am happy to help others and trust God to help me.

Transformation of our hearts is possible when God is the catalyst.

# EIGHT

# In God We Trust

## Self vs. God

The Alpha Man Code preaches, "In Self we trust." Alpha men rely on our wits, persistence and will power to meet our goals. If self-reliance is such a brilliant strategy, why do we struggle with significance and question our purpose? Why do our relationships falter so frequently?

Determining our need to change does not ensure we have the capacity to create transformation. A powerful will can't realign deep seeded motivations and attitudes.

If we can't trust Self to create this level of change, what can we trust as the source?

In a story I mentioned earlier, Dr. King said, "I am at the end of my power. I have nothing left. I have come to the point where I can't face it alone."[29] Dr. King recognized the limitations of Self. He acknowledged his lack of strength to persevere. On his own, he could not overcome the hardship and persecution he and his followers faced.

All men have felt powerless. The Alpha Man Code says, "Suck it up," or "Keep cool." Neither approach addresses the problem or our fear. Dr. King identified and accessed an alternative.

"At that moment," he continued, "I experienced the presence of God as I have never experienced Him before. It seemed as though I could hear the quiet assurance of an inner voice saying, 'Stand up for righteousness, stand up for truth; and God will be at your side forever.' Almost at once my fears began to go. My uncertainty disappeared. I was ready to face anything."

Dr. King turned to God and his fear disappeared. His doubt vanished. At the end of his powers, Dr. King was empowered. **He was ready to face any foe with God at his side.** *God* provided the fortitude Dr. King required to continue the Civil Rights movement.

Can God empower any man? What is the rationale for placing our trust in God instead of Self?

Dr. King did not suspend his intellect when choosing to follow God, nor was he a weak man down on his luck. One of the most influential leaders of our time possessed the wisdom to put Self on the bench and call on a more powerful source. **In the Alpha Man vs. God debate, Dr. Martin Luther King chose God.**

Dr. King knew these biblical truths: God is trustworthy and God is eternal. Even men unfamiliar with scripture are familiar with these concepts. We see this message daily—every U.S. dollar is printed with the words "In God We Trust."

What does it mean to trust God?

Many of us are familiar with the biblical account of David and Goliath. David, a King of Israel and one of the greatest military leaders in history, was just a shepherd boy when he killed the giant Goliath by slinging a stone. What gave this pipsqueak the courage to face a bloodthirsty, seven-foot warrior with a sword the size of a surfboard? Was David crazy? Was he cocky? Was he high on pasture grass or rock lichen?

David trusted God. Volunteering to fight Goliath, the youthful David said, "The Lord who delivered me from the paw of the lion and the paw of the bear will deliver me from the hand of this Philistine."

David's defeat of Goliath doesn't make sense. It isn't reasonable. However, David had something Goliath hadn't considered. David did not fight alone. Though he walked onto the battlefield by himself, he had a covenant with God. **David trusted God was at his side.** And he slew Goliath.

Here's a more contemporary story. After beating the Yankees in game six of the 2004 ALCS Red Sox pitcher Curt Schilling, bloody sock and all, was interviewed on national television. "Tonight, God did something amazing," Schilling said after one of the gutsiest performances in sports history. "I knew that I wasn't going to be able to do this alone. I just prayed for the strength to go out there tonight and compete, and [God] gave me that."

Schilling did not feel alone. God was with him on the mound and gave him the strength to win a pivotal playoff game.

Relying on God's power does not mean all our prayers will come to pass. God delivers what we *need* not simply what we *want*. We trust God's will is in our best interest whether or not we land a big deal or win a key game. What is most important is not the outcome but the fact that God is walking alongside us.

**Our hope is not what God can do *for* us, but what He can do *with* us.** God uses the gifts and skills He provides us to carry out His design for us. This is the purpose we seek. This is the identity we wish to uncover. Yielding to His will provides meaning and fulfillment.

Wouldn't it feel better if you weren't alone in the trenches at work when your portfolio heads south, or have a bad quarter, or business flounders? Wouldn't you be relieved if someone offered sound advice when your marriage fractures, your kids get sick, and mortgage and car payments suck you dry? Wouldn't it be great to have somebody listen to your woes without judging or trying to fix you?

**God is with you.**

# The Redeemer

I had pre-conceived notions about God. My perspective was based on murky recollections from Sunday school and second-hand information from friends. I remembered a Bible full of stories with moral lessons and happy endings. To me, these ancient legends and fables about God were no more real than Zeus, Apollo, or Poseidon of Greek mythology or the Roman gods Jupiter and Mars.

God seemed to be an impersonal, gray-bearded deity residing in the clouds. He condemned mankind in His booming voice, assailing our sins and disobedience. Was my viewpoint accurate? How would I know?

I did some homework. With all the hours I spent researching stocks or my Final Four picks, the least I could do was put in time to figure out who God *really* is. What I found shocked me.

God is an artist, architect, mathematician, and scientist. He is a brilliant leader, wise judge, compassionate counselor, and caring father. He is holy, true, and forever consistent. A fascinating paradox, God is powerful, mighty and to be revered, yet loving and merciful. He holds us accountable for our actions while granting forgiveness when we falter.

**God offers redemption.** His love and grace enable us to put our past to rest. God cares about the condition of our heart, not the title on our business card or the thickness of our wallet. Accomplishments and accolades don't matter as much as altruism and love for others.

God actively pursues relationships with us. Sounds crazy, right? Think of it this way: God, the all-knowing Almighty wants to have a conversation. It's as if He walked into our home, plopped down in our favorite chair, clicked off the ballgame and asks, "What's going on, son?"

Academy Award-winning actor Denzel Washington said, "There is no doubt about it, I have felt the hand of God throughout my life."

**God is deeply engaged with each of us individually:** the joys we feel, tribulations we struggle through, heaviness on our hearts, the good, the bad, and the ugly. If you feel unworthy of a relationship with God, think again. If you believe you have crossed Him too often, reconsider. If you assume He doesn't have time for you and your petty issues, give Him a ring. God will answer your call.


## Divine Design

Alpha men want independence. We want command and authority over our future. We want to fulfill our own plan, not follow a script ginned up by someone else. We want, we want, we want.

**We are trying to become the men we *want* to be rather than becoming the men God designed us to be.** This is why we feel empty, afraid and disconnected.

The horizon of our own self-interest constrains us. Our wants and appetites blind us to broader opportunities. Our vision for our life is too narrow. Dr. Billy Graham said, "The smallest package in the world is a human being all wrapped up in himself." I don't want to be a small man. Do you?

Legendary football coach Vince Lombardi set the standard for modern day coaches. The NFL championship trophy is named after him not just because of his incredible winning record. As Packer great Jerry Kramer put it, "He made us all better than we thought we could be."

Lombardi saw potential in his players they could not see themselves. He challenged them to do more than what they wanted. He stretched them beyond what felt comfortable. And they became better men for it.

God has a leg up on Lombardi. Imagine what He has in mind for us. God has a BIG vision for each of our lives. He helps us to be better than we imagine. If men trust God and rely on Him, we *can* make a difference.

One of my favorite biblical passages is from the Old Testament prophet Jeremiah, who speaks on God's behalf: "For I know the plans I have for you; plans to prosper and to grow, plans to give you hope and a future."

**God has a plan for us.** No matter who we are or where we think we stand with God, He authors a specific purpose for each of our lives. We don't have to start the next Google, break the all-time home run record, or create a blockbuster movie to make an impact. God can use us right where we are to help change the world.

Our independent hearts and minds chafe under His authority, but God's wisdom is infinitely greater than ours. The challenges and suffering we face in life can undercut our faith in God, but they are opportunities to strengthen our relationship with Him.

You're probably scratching your head thinking, *Why would this almighty, all-knowing, more-powerful-than-Oz character need my help to carry out His plan?*

That is a great question!

Did God foresee trouble with His future creation and require our assistance? Did some new technology stump Him? The rotary engine? A portable TV you can slip into your pocket? Less filling beer that tastes great? Soy nuts?

Actually, God doesn't need our help. He just wants to be with us.

I remember wandering into the garage when my dad worked on the car. I didn't know the difference between a socket wrench and a spark plug, but dad called me over to lend a hand. With a few instructions, I was in up to my elbows in manifolds and motor oil. Man, there was nothing more exhilarating than putting the wing nut on the top of the air filter and wiping my grimy hands on my flanks like a real mechanic. Dad gave me a prideful grin and a slap on the shoulder. After such an experience, I was sky high for a week. And so was dad.

My dad didn't *need* me to finish the job—it simply pleased him to spend time together. It's the same way with God. He doesn't *need* us to fulfill His plan. He *wants* to spend time with us. He wants to slap us on the shoulder and say, "Atta boy, Champ."

God pursues a relationship with each of us. Understanding this truth makes us look at everything differently.

## Power of Grace

Intellectually, we understand heart transformation. While it is a stretch, we can come to grips with God being a catalyst. But how do we actually experience this change?

Naturally, alpha men can turn to a rock star for the answer. Bono wrestled with this issue. He ascribed to the concept of karma, an idea that makes sense to results-oriented men like us.

"It's clear to me that karma is at the very heart of the universe. I'm absolutely sure of it," Bono wrote. "And yet, along comes this idea called grace to upend all that 'as you reap, so you will sow' stuff. Grace defies reason and logic. Love interrupts, if you like, the consequences of your actions, which in my case is very good news indeed, because I've done a lot of stupid stuff."[30]

Grace is unmerited mercy, undeserved release from our debts. Unconditional forgiveness falls outside the realm of common sense. What's more, **God extends grace to any and all of His followers regardless of their past or future transgressions.**

There is a price to pay for our wrongdoings. Justice must be served. How does God strike this critical balance of judgment and mercy?

Bono continues, "[Jesus] took on the sins of the world, so that what we put out did not come back to us, and that our sinful nature does not reap the obvious death. That's the point. It should keep us humbled...It's not our own good works that get us through the gates of heaven."

We receive the gift of grace because God made the ultimate sacrifice: "For God so loved the world that he gave his one and only son so that whoever believes in him shall not perish but have eternal life."[31]

God gave up His son to intercede on our behalf. And Jesus fulfilled our sentence willingly. By dying on the cross, Jesus endured *our* judgment. He died so *we* would be saved. Jesus paid the bill for *our* lifetime of transgressions. **Because of Jesus' sacrifice, we are forgiven.**

As a result, we are in good standing with God. Regardless of how rude or cruel we have been (or will be), despite our debauchery, God loves us.

This truth melts our hearts. When we acknowledge the depths of our selfishness and witness the extent of God's unselfishness, the stranglehold of pride and superiority is broken.

## We Are Sons

Christ's sacrifice is not merely a pardon. Our gift from God goes beyond unmerited favor. We are not just in good standing, **we are God's sons!**

In his letter to the Galatians Paul explains an enlightening part of the Gospel truth: "So you are no longer a slave, but a son and since you are a son, God has made you also an heir."[32] We are adopted into God's family. He is a Father to all of His followers.

What does being a son of God mean for us?

As a dad, I can relate to the power of family ties. I am amazed at how my heart aches for my boys. At times, they disobey, or worse, ignore me. No matter how they behave, my love for them endures—it is not conditional.

**God is our Father and His love is unconditional.** Whether we believe in Him or not, whether we are indifferent or hostile, God loves us. We may be angry with Him because things don't go our way. We disregard His advice or disobey Him completely. Regardless of our past or our future, God stands by us. He is more willing to forgive us for our transgressions than we are to admit our mistakes.

God watches over us. He thinks about us constantly and looks out for our best interests. God mends our brokenness. He heals wounds of abandonment. He lifts our burden of loneliness. While we will continue to fail and make mistakes, God forgives us. With open arms, he invites us in as though saying "I am here for you, always."

Gentlemen, we are God's sons. We are redeemed from our past. When Jesus stepped in to take our judgment, he bore our sentence. All our transgressions have been paid in full. We have been liberated and are right with God.

We don't have to prove ourselves anymore. Results don't matter. Performance is immaterial. We don't have to validate our masculinity with boasting or macho nonsense. We can stop relying on external labels to define us. Our new name is son of God.

When we question, "Am I worthy?" God answers, "Yes you are, my son."

## Experiencing Transformation

If you're curious what it would be like to live as a son of God and interested in exploring a more profound relationship with Him, consider these four principles:

- God loves us and created us to know Him personally. We were destined for a life of meaning and fulfillment
- All people are selfish by nature and separated from God. Therefore, none can know Him personally. We can't earn our way into God's good graces by our words or works.

- Jesus is God's only provision for our selfish nature. Jesus is the bridge that spans our relationship with God. Through Jesus alone we can know God personally.
- We must individually receive Jesus as Savior and Lord. When we ask Jesus to redeem our lives we are reunited with God forever.

When you are ready to build your relationship with God consider this prayer.

*God, I want to know you personally. Thank you sending your Son to die on the cross for my sins. Please forgive all my transgressions and give me eternal life. I open the door of my life and receive Jesus as my Savior and Lord. Help me follow your will and trust my life to you.* **God, make me the kind of man you want me to be.**

If this represents the desire of your heart, find a quiet place. Ask God into your life. Don't worry, He is listening. He is waiting to say, "Welcome to the family, son."

# NINE

# Character
# Is the New Currency

## A New Standard

**Men model other men.** We take our cues from leaders we respect and admire. We seek examples, not experts—demonstrations rather than explanations.

Bono suggests the ideal model of character: **"If only we could be a bit more like [Jesus], the world would be transformed."**[33]

Why would Bono—iconoclast lead singer of the band U2, a man of worldwide fame and immense wealth, who defines cool with his blue-fly shades, and fights for Third World relief—find Jesus heroic?

Jesus is the new standard for men. He modeled perfect character. Jesus is stamped with the holy nature of God. His actions could not have resulted from conforming to a set of moral codes or ethical statues. No behavioral modification technique or training class guided Him. He was ingrained with God's divine design for character.

God was "well pleased" with Jesus' character, not the growth of His carpentry business or His popularity with the ladies. God's love for His Son was absolute and never ending. The connection between Father and Son fortified Jesus through the conflict and persecution He suffered as well as his success and fanfare. Jesus remained righteous in the face of temptation and infallible in the face of danger—even death on a cross.

**The source of Jesus' character is a covenant with God.** It is the outflow of an *unconditional* and *eternal* relationship. Covenantal character is God-oriented and other-centric. It is as much about relational excellence as moral distinction. A transformed heart is made manifest through interactions with others.

Jesus embodied covenantal character by trusting the untrustworthy. The nature of His relationship with God enabled Jesus to love the unlovable. He had compassion for the oppressed. To outcasts, He offered grace. **Jesus saw others not as they were but who they could be.**

The example Jesus set is one that *all* men can understand and *any* man can implement.

## The Divinity of Jesus

Jesus is one of the most controversial figures in history. The mere mention of His name can spur heated debate. Misperception and misinformation abound. Many people question His divinity and in particular His virgin birth, the resurrection and His claim to be the Son of God.

"I would like to ask [Jesus] if He was indeed virgin born," said talk show host Larry King, who regularly conducts discussions of theology and religion. "Because the answer to that question would define history."

Since history is measured by years since Jesus' birth, perhaps this is the case.

Some concede that Jesus was a great teacher, moral leader or prophet like Elijah, Muhammad, Buddha, or Confucius. Bono disputes this perspective saying:

"Christ doesn't allow you that. He doesn't let you off the hook. Christ says: *No. I'm not saying I'm a teacher, don't call me teacher. I'm not saying I'm a prophet. I'm saying: 'I'm the Messiah.' I'm saying: 'I am God incarnate.'* And people say: *No, no, please, just be a prophet. A prophet, we can take. You're a bit eccentric. We've had John the Baptist eating locusts and wild honey, we can handle that. But don't mention the 'M' word! Because, you know, we're gonna have to crucify you.* And he goes: *No, no. I know you're expecting me to come back with an army, and set you free from these creeps, but actually I am the Messiah.* At this point, everyone starts staring at their shoes, and says: *Oh, my God, he's gonna keep saying this.* **So what you're left with is: either Christ was who He said He was—the Messiah—or a complete nutcase."**

Bono is right—we cannot be on the fence regarding Jesus. Perhaps that is what makes Jesus so contentious a figure. There is no middle ground or room for compromise.

According to the Bible, Jesus is God incarnate. Being part of God's Trinity made man does not mean that He wasn't fully human. Jesus lived, His heart beat, He breathed, ate, and aged. When sentenced to death by crucifixion, His body was torn and His life ended. Then, Jesus was resurrected.

By defeating death, Jesus gives us hope for eternal life. He is the example of this supernatural reality.

The resurrection is difficult to understand. When researching the validity of this truth, three questions stand out. First, if Jesus was *not* resurrected what happened to His body after He died? Second, how do you explain the numerous eyewitness testimonies of the resurrected Christ chronicled in the Bible? Third, why are countless followers unwilling to renounce Jesus when facing punishment of death for their belief?

**I believe Jesus is the Son of God.**

But I am not you. And I would never be so patronizing or pretentious to try convincing you of these biblical truths. Carry out your own assessment. Do the research. Speak to a pastor or Rabbi. Pull together some buddies and discuss the eyewitness accounts of the gospels. They provide the ultimate inside story on Jesus' coming, ministry, death, and resurrection. Draw your own conclusions. You may be surprised by what you discover. You will want to understand the true nature of Jesus.

## The Real Jesus

The image I had of Jesus was meek and mild, a gentle lamb of a man. Innumerable paintings depict Jesus with soft features and angelic, feminine expressions. What alpha man wants to be like that?

Unlike other role models, **Jesus is the one man who looks better under close examination.** The more you understand who He is, and why and how He lived, the more your perspective will change. His words are provocative. His actions are shocking. He was a man on a mission, a valiant leader and champion of the little guy, who sacrificed His life for what He believed.

Movies are littered with hard-nosed guys. Ruthlessly determined and driven characters like Scarface, the outlaw Josey Wales, William Wallace, and Rocky reinforce an Alpha Man Code that equates toughness with masculinity: walk it off; suck it up; win at all costs. While many guys are infatuated with these characters' machismo, for me nothing defines a real man more than Jesus' actions during His crucifixion.

In his blockbuster film *The Passion of the Christ,*[34] Mel Gibson focused on the brutality Jesus endured on His way to the cross. The violence inflicted on Him is so unnerving audiences turn their heads away.

Close to death from a horrific flogging, Jesus was brought before Pontius Pilate. The Roman governor knew Jesus was innocent of the charges against Him and demanded a response. Jesus chose not answer. "Don't you realize I have the power to either free you or crucify you?" Pilate asked.

Jesus understood the agony he would face. Yet when Pilate offered a reprieve, He remained steadfast. He did not complain, plead His case, or beg for mercy. Resolute to fulfill His calling, He glowered, "You would have no power over me if it were not given to you from above." Pilate was stunned. Reluctantly, he turned Jesus over to the mob shouting for His execution.

Jesus voluntarily suffered persecution and death on a cross to save the rest of us from the consequences of our sin. What man, no matter how tough, would *willingly* submit to such torture? Jesus could have come down off the cross at any time yet he made himself helpless and vulnerable for us. We are *that* important to Him.

His actions serve as a model and an inspiration for others, including *The Passion's* filmmaker. "I came to a difficult point in my life," said Gibson in an interview with ABC's Diane Sawyer.[35] "Meditating on Christ's sufferings, on His Passion, got me through it. Life is hard, and we all get wounded by it— I was no exception. I went to the wounds of Christ in order to cure my own wounds."

Relentless pursuit of one's personal agenda is not heroic. Intimidation does not make a man brave. Any bully can evoke fear. **A willingness to suffer on behalf of others is true humanity.** And Jesus made the ultimate sacrifice so each of us could have hope through eternal life.

## Standing Up For Others

Influential men represent those whose voices go unheard. Dr. Martin Luther King spoke for justice, defying the bigotry of unjust authorities and practices. Gandhi united the Indian population, including the scorned untouchables, and challenged the oppression of British rulers.

Jesus' impact was even greater.

First, Jesus was an advocate for the forgotten. He gave hope to the destitute. He reached out to the physically lame, emotionally broken, socially mute and spiritually lost. Jesus taught, consoled, dined, and wept with them. He understood their pain because of the injustices He would suffer.

Second, Jesus took on the establishment of His day. He called out the ruling class, exposing their insincerity and self-serving motives. Neither their tactics nor death threats intimidated Him.

The Pharisees were the Jewish elite during the Roman occupation. These high priests professed to be godly men, yet they abused their religious power and browbeat their Israeli countrymen.

A biblical passage relates how Jesus exposed their hypocrisy at a meal in a Pharisees' home: "You Pharisees are so careful to clean the outside of the cup and dish, but inside you are still filthy—full of greed and wickedness!" He continued, "So give to the needy what you greedily possess and you will be clean all over."[36]

The Pharisees were insulted and furious. Jesus did not back down. At the temple shortly thereafter, Jesus warned thousands against the duplicity of these religious noblemen.

"Do not follow [the Pharisees'] example. For they don't practice what they teach. They crush you with impossible religious demands and never lift a finger to help ease the burden." Continuing to address the crowd Jesus said, "Everything they do is for show...And how they love to sit at the head table at the banquets and in the most prominent seats in the synagogues! They enjoy the attention they get on the streets and they enjoy being called, 'Rabbi.'"[37]

The stand Jesus made for others touched the hearts of the masses. They flocked to him, trading in a life of hopelessness for an eternity with God. As a result, a powerful movement spread across the region upending the power of the Jewish rulers and, eventually, the Roman Empire.

Jesus' influence stemmed from His unconditional love for others. "Love is the only way to win the free response of men," wrote Robert Coleman, a distinguished professor from Gordon-Conwell Seminary. "And this is possible only by the presence of [God] within the heart."[38] The love of God in Jesus' heart was the source of His influence.

## Servant Heart

While Jesus' transformational leadership is inspiring, not all of us can initiate a major social or political movement. An incident at the Last Supper provides a powerful and practical application for any of us.[39]

Jesus' disciples arranged for an upper room to enjoy their Passover feast. Because of the dusty desert roads of the region and the sandals people wore, foot washing was a common custom. A good host provided a slave or servant to execute the grungy task.

Before dinner, Jesus rose from His seat. He wrapped a towel around His waist and poured water in a basin. Calling His disciples one by one, he fell to his knees and washed their feet.

To His stunned disciples he explained, "Since I, the Lord and Teacher, have washed your feet, you ought to wash each other's feet. **I have given you an example to follow. Do as I have done to you.**"

Jesus didn't lecture. He got down on the floor and modeled how to serve. Can you imagine a CEO heading to the basement to launder a janitor's uniform? Or a Senator waiting at a Chinese joint to pick up take-out for his interns?

The depth of humility and purity of character Jesus demonstrated serves as the new standard for men. While we cannot attain His level of righteousness, we can express our thanks for His grace by serving others. With the love of God in our hearts, each of us is capable of similar acts of compassion and service.

Imagine the impact an example like this could have at work. We can minister to colleagues, asking the extra question to address issues below the surface. By focusing on peers' strengths rather than their weaknesses, we can help them develop and encourage them to reach their professional goals.

At home, a more selfless heart will drastically alter how we interact with our wife and children. We will share the joy and look for help from a relationship with God. With Jesus as our role model, character rather than competency is our new currency.

## TEN

# A New Power Source

## Synthetic Hearts

You might be thinking, *Okay, okay, I get it. If God and others come first, my heart is transformed. With Jesus as my example, I can live an abundant life. All my problems are solved, right? The male gender is saved. Bring on world hunger.*

Not so fast. Here's the issue: **the default love of every man's heart is Self.** Since the fall of man, this is our nature. Self will always be our first priority. No matter how much fortitude we apply, our hearts will revert to the original factory settings.

Many men experience significant change through twelve-step programs, rehab, marital counseling, or anger management seminars. Effective techniques can break longstanding habits. The effects of these approaches are limited, though, by their inability to cure selfishness.

Many drinkers start smoking; smokers start overeating; over-eaters start purging. When we don't address the root cause of abuse, it will worm its way from one part of our lives to the next.

Mere behavioral modification produces a synthetic heart. This vinyl-sided replica is not radically altered from the inside out. A synthetic heart is merely ethically confined or morally restrained. We enclose our impulses and corral our carnal desires rather than deal with underlying causes. Our internal governance mechanisms help us act appropriately for a while but are not robust enough to prevent us from falling back into old habits.

With synthetic hearts, we may do the right thing for the wrong reasons. **Virtuous behavior can come from selfish motivations.** Any man can be moral or just for a season. We can be compassionate or courteous on cue. We frequent church, quit profanity, write checks for the poor, serve meals to the homeless—all good deeds which can result from selfishness.

I added God to my world and expected big changes. Unfortunately, God was not *big* in my life. Applying an alpha man approach, I formed God in my own image and squeezed Him into my lifestyle. I incorporated appealing components of His biblical canon but chucked the rest of God's doctrine as irrelevant or outdated. Giving away ten percent of gross income was "unrealistic" with the high cost of living in New York. No premarital sex was "old-fashioned." Surrendering to God's will was "unsuitable" for this highly-educated HBS alum.

The god I created in my mind was a pygmy who couldn't transform a gnat. Thus, the changes in my life were only incremental.

Until God became a reality rather than an intellectual concept, I stalled. I had to accept the truth about who God really was, not entertain a fantasy about who I wanted Him to be.

Deciding we don't like the consequences of gravity doesn't mean Newton's law does not exist. The same is true for God: a man's uncertainty about His existence does not alter the truth of His being.

How big is God in your life? Is He first in your heart or is He fire insurance for when troubles arise?

Do you attend church because it is the "right thing to do" or because you can't wait to thank God for what He has done for you? Do you tithe to the poor because you are broken with compassion for their plight or because it's a tax write-off?

God doesn't care about our religion, He wants a relationship. He doesn't need us to be enlightened by new teaching.

God wants us to be deeply humbled by our own brokenness and thawed by the depth of His love for us. He doesn't need us to act like His followers. He wants us to pray passionately, mentor and minister to others, and serve with joy in our hearts.

**To experience transformation, we must be willing to mold ourselves around God rather than the other way around.**

Men will fill our heart deficit according to Self or Spirit, Alpha Man or God. Who we choose to follow and the steps we take to make this a reality are vital.

How do we change the focus of our hearts from Self to God? There is only one solution: a supernatural transformation.

## Paradox of Surrender

Does surrendering to God's will for our lives make us meek or desperate? Why would any alpha man volunteer to take this step?

Let's make a couple things clear. First, **yielding to God doesn't make you a wimp.** It is one of the most heroic acts you can undertake. Surrendering control is courageous. You must be brave to swallow your pride and remove Self from authority.

Johnny Cash said, "The prosperity of life will cage us, the surrender to Christ will set us free." Paradoxically, submitting to God's will is both liberating and empowering.

Second, transformation of the heart is not like winning the lottery. None of the guys mentioned in this book experienced an explosion of net worth resulting from their relationship with God. No talent or fame engulfed them. In fact, several of us saw our external circumstances *deteriorate.*

God is not a vending machine distributing the right job or the right relationship on request. Nor is He the Godfather, granting favors and sending henchmen to claim a pound of flesh from our enemies. God doesn't magically bail us out of debt or fix an unwanted pregnancy. And we're not talking about "The Force" or some cosmic energy source that provides us power over others.

God promises abundance of life, not material wealth. By following Him, we can have a life of peace and joy.

Third, a relationship with God is a journey, not a doorway. Connecting with Him is a daily battle requiring our *full* engagement. It requires commitment and effort, just like relationships with our wives, kids, peers, and clients.


## Our Personal Wingman

Performance-first workplaces can be exhausting. The continuous expectation to deliver improvements offers little rest. We can be treated unfairly or unjustly, making us angry and frustrated. We wonder why we bother developing character and integrity when others don't value or respect them.

God anticipated this challenge. He did not abandon us when His Son was crucified. "Because you are sons," wrote Paul, "God sent the Spirit of [God] into our hearts."[40]

This Spirit of God (a.k.a. Holy Spirit, Holy Ghost, Spirit of Life) is part of God's Trinity: God the Father, Jesus the Son, and the Holy Spirit. The Holy Spirit is our counselor, illuminating truth and alerting us when we damage our relationship with God.

The Holy Spirit is like our own personal wingman. He walks alongside us day and night. **The Spirit teaches and guides us, helping us focus on the important instead of the urgent.** We are less apprehensive about fluctuating conditions because our wingman illuminates the big picture and keeps us properly balanced.

The German philosopher Johann Goethe wrote, "Treat a man as he is, and he will remain as he is; treat a man as he can be and should be and he will become as he can and should be." The Spirit sees our potential and helps us discern what God

98

designed us to be. He encourages and exhorts us to pursue our relationship with God beyond what we think possible.

A scene from the movie *Hoosiers*[41] helped me sort out this concept. When the boys from Hickory entered the fifteen thousand-seat gymnasium before the state championship game, they stood with mouths agape. Coach Norman Dale (Gene Hackman) sensed his team buckling under pressure. The size of the crowd, the media, and the enormity of the game intimidated his team. Their distraction threatened their chances for victory.

Standing on the foul line of the empty arena, Coach Dale pulled a tape measure from his pocket. "Buddy, hold this under the backboard," he instructed. The tape was stretched between them. "How long?"

"Fifteen feet."

"Fifteen feet," Dale repeated. Next, he told Ollie to get on Strap's shoulders. He measured the distance from the rim to the floor. "How far?" Coach Dale asked.

"Ten feet."

"Ten feet." Everyone gazed at Coach Dale curiously. What was his point?

"Gentlemen," he explained, "I think you will find these are the exact same measurements as in our gym back in Hickory." The recovery of his team was instantaneous. Coach Dale reconnected them to the familiarity of their home court.

With the Holy Spirit as God's presence dwelling in our hearts, we always enjoy a home-court advantage. We have a sense of familiarity even in the unfamiliar. We feel comfortable despite difficult circumstances. Even when things are not going our way, we are confident we will prevail. Our personal wingman helps keep our faith in God's provision.

## Strength to Overcome

God's Spirit helps us in areas of our life where we stumble. For me, the major hurdle was forgiveness.

My first marriage failed. There, I said it.

The divorce is a black mark I must live with. It was a long, tortuous experience, and did not end when we signed the court papers. Blaming my ex-wife for the demise of our relationship was an easier route than admitting my own fault. Her behavior was not the only reason for our split-up. I had a role. I just preferred to play the victim.

Because of biblical precedent for our divorce, the church exonerated me. I felt vindicated, yet I wanted restitution.

Like any of us who feel wronged, I stepped behind the judge's bench. I felt qualified to determine my ex-wife's guilt and issue her sentence. When God did not strike her down in the manner I prescribed, I grew angry. I thought, *There is an injustice here! Somebody must pay for my pain!*

On my own, I was not strong enough to put this bitterness and resentment behind me. Thankfully, I had somewhere to turn. Not by might, nor by power but by My Spirit," God stated through the prophet Zechariah. Forgiveness is possible through the power of God within us.

Just as Dr. King was empowered by God's Spirit, so was I. With the Spirit of God inhabiting our hearts, we are fortified with the clout of the Almighty. God enables us to turn away from all that is destructive in our lives. When our will falters, the Spirit comes through. God sustains us.

The more we ask for help, the more prepared we are to accept it. That is a primary reason for prayer: to ask God for help. With the New Man Code, we willingly reach out to God for His assistance, preparing ourselves for His aid—which He gives in unexpected forms.

The Spirit enabled me to forgive. He pointed me to Jesus. God's Son bore the pain of my transgressions on the cross. I was due to be punished but Jesus took the hit for me. And He asked nothing in return. Every time I ruminated about the injustice in my first marriage, the Spirit of God took me back to this truth: ***Jesus* died for me.** As my bitterness faded, I remembered, **Jesus *died* for me**. I let go of my anger when I realized **Jesus died for *me.***

Finally, I was released from my own bondage. The power of God's love healed my heart. I was freed from the acrimony of my failure. The Spirit opened my eyes to the new life God mapped out for me. He incorporated my suffering into His plan.

At the time, it was impossible to fathom how my divorce could be used by God to bless others. In hindsight, it makes perfect sense. When I sit and talk with guys struggling with marital problems I can speak from experience. That is valuable to them.

Through the power of the Spirit, God draws me to Him and helps me help others.

# ELEVEN

# Investing in Others

## A Fresh Start

God, eternal life, the Holy Spirit, purpose, identity, supernatural transformation, character, and influence—these are some major concepts to chew on. Wow! How do we keep it all straight? What are the practical applications?

The New Man Code is challenging but I am committed to make it come alive. I am encouraged that God wants to build a relationship with us and can use each of us right where we are to impact those around us.

Investing in others was a logical place for me to start. Developing character, particularly integrity, was an area I could tackle as well. Relational excellence and personal equity were new to me but made sense. Other men in my circle made similar pledges.

The paths of the guys who shared their stories in this book are akin to my own. Each of us exchanged a self-directed life for a God-directed life. We ceded God authority, trusting He will reform our hearts. Building a relationship with God and surrendering to His will became a simple choice, the only one guaranteeing lasting change.

In college, my buddies and I used to listen to Paul Harvey's radio broadcasts every day. His melodic voice spun a tale that always built to a cliffhanger; then he would announce, "And now for the *rest* of the story." Then, Harvey revealed an unknown fact or hidden subplot, illuminating the lives and events he described.

For Doug, Billy, John, Seth, Jered, Stephen, Matt and yours truly, the *rest* of the story began at the same place. Despite different heritages, vocations, and spiritual backgrounds, we experienced similar transformations.

None of us planned the winding course our lives took. We didn't expect the pitfalls and setbacks we experienced. We thought we had the skills and the will to get through any situation unscathed. We found that driving, pushing, and coercing our way through life didn't yield desirable results. Emptiness, fear, and isolation controlled us.

Conforming to conventional norms was politically correct but emotionally corrosive. When we could no longer tolerate the Alpha Man Code status quo, we questioned the foundations of our worldviews. Taking time to reflect, we entertained new perspectives. **Each of us willingly surrendered to the will of God rather Self.** In the Alpha Man vs. God debate, we chose God.

An encounter with Jesus opened our eyes to a new perspective. Today, John spends time with homeless people—not just serving food or donating money to help, but sitting and talking with them. Doug and Matt are back with their wives and their marriages are flourishing. Jered helps stabilize a fledgling church. Stephen hosts dinners for friends to discuss their beliefs and reasons for them. Seth spends time in fellowship with other men and Billy mentors young professionals.

These guys are not paid for these activities. **Their investment in others is an overflow of their changed hearts.** Most will tell you it is a joy to share their time and talents with others—that, in fact, they are blessed as much as the people they aid. These guys aren't trying to win community service awards or tout their kind-heartedness. No boss or local leader pressures them to serve. They do it because their transformed hearts move them to do so.

For me, the turning point came when I admitted I was lost. The path of accomplishment and material gain left me unfulfilled and isolated. Self could not overcome the chaos and violence of the workplace or the complex emotional underpinnings of marriage. I was not smart enough to figure life out on my own. My will caved in to the temptations of personal glory. Truthfully, I was not in control.

Life changed when I turned over command. Surrendering to God's plan instead of my self-designed scheme was the wisest decision I ever made. God uncovered better uses for my skills and gifts than I ever imagined. Now, I get to huddle with guys like me, men who seem like they have all the answers but are actually filled with questions. God directs my time and energies, but I'm never weary.

One proverb instructs, "Many are the plans in a man's heart, but it is the Lord's purpose that prevails."[42] Pursuing God's purpose rather than my own provides meaning and passion for my life.

## Men of Integrity

One way God challenges me is developing integrity. This is a word bandied about with lots of politically correct platitudes. I find men often misunderstand its meaning and do not hold themselves to high standards.

The word comes from the combined Latin modifier "in" and the root "tangere," meaning untouched, or wholeness and undivided. This means our inner life and outer life are synchronized. We are balanced. Our private world and our public persona are consistent. Actions and behaviors at work are the same as at home, and vice-versa. We treat those closest to us with the same respect and courtesy as our best customers.

"Integrity is the basis of trust,"[43] wrote leadership sage Warren Bennis. To be trustworthy, we must be men of integrity. Our wives and kids are looking for a man who is

105

authentic about his feelings and reliable in his actions. Clients and colleagues want us to be straightforward and accountable.

In his book *Integrity,* Stephen Carter argues that men are capable of preserving integrity in our lives.[44] He posits that maintaining integrity is an ongoing effort, based on the following behavior:

- discerning between right and wrong
- remaining steadfast to commitments
- being unashamed of doing what is right

Integrity is rarely a question of awareness. Most times, we know when we are dishonest or deceptive. Even as children we sense right from wrong, complaining when "it's not fair!"

So why do men compromise our integrity? How can our word be of such little value to us? The problem is our abacus is busted. Men's mental cost/benefit calculations are wrong. We believe the potential payoff warrants any risk. Our shortsightedness blinds us to the depth of consequences.

"There is nothing concealed that will not be disclosed, or hidden that will not be made known," Jesus said. "What you have said in the dark will be heard in the daylight and what you have whispered in the ear in the inner rooms will be proclaimed from the roofs."[45]

**God sees *everything*.** Nothing gets by Him, absolutely nothing. He recognizes our *intentions* as well as our actions. Next time you consider violating your integrity, put the following assumptions into your risk/reward evaluation:

- You *will* be caught
- You will pay the *maximum* penalty

Jesus points out how this equation changes when minor transgressions result in major consequences. If losing your job for fudging an expense report were certain, would you act differently? If flirting with an attractive office assistant alienated your kids forever, would you reconsider? If a jail sentence and public humiliation were the end result of ripping off your insurance company, would it be worth the gain?

This is not a 'scared straight' tactic, just realignment of perspectives on breaching our integrity. When we cross this line, we're not in possession of our whole selves. We separate ourselves from God, threatening to do so eternally.

Jesus said, "You will know the truth and the truth will set you free."[46] Advancing our level of integrity is a practical step any man can implement immediately.


## Relational Excellence

Excellence is a foundational principle for alpha men. Our credibility at work is a function of our competence, expertise, and commitment to maximize the bottom line. We are diligent and vigorous about doing our job exceptionally well.

Unfortunately, we rarely apply the same commitment to excellence in our relationships. Alpha men are masters of transactional relationships. Such conditional arrangements enable us to stay in control and bail out when necessary.

If we examine any relationship, we see that interdependence rather than independence builds trust with others. In his recent book, Bethel Seminary professor Mark McCloskey wrote, "Character is less what I do when no one is watching, and more what I do when someone is interacting with me."[47] Character, then, is refined through the engagement and conflicts of relationships.

McCloskey explains that God offers ultimate trust in the ultimate relationship. Knowing God is with us at any hour and will forgive us no matter what our sins affords us the strength to build and maintain relationships.

**Relational excellence is a cornerstone of the New Man Code.** Our relationship with God will inform and serve as a model for our relationships with others. Instead of forming win-win exchanges, we choose to give of ourselves freely and build a rich connection. Relational excellence both fosters and contributes to our ability to be authentic, accepting, and available.

Trust is non-negotiable in personal interactions: economic, political, social, and familial. We can't buy trust; we must earn it. Personal trustworthiness is essential for building relationships.

Trustworthiness begins when we trust God. We stop trying to manipulate our circumstances and rely on Him and His promises to provide for us. We renounce Self and grant grace to others.

"We love because He first loved us," wrote the apostle John.[48] We can love others because God loves us. With Jesus, our identity is beloved son. This personal tie to God leads us to serve others.

Character built on God's unconditional love centers on trust, not tenacity. It relies on faith, not force. God's trustworthiness enhances and strengthens our own.

Relational excellence at home means we commit the time and attention to ensure connection with our family is *outstanding*. We openly discuss the challenges we face in our marriages: communication, conflict resolution, intimacy, and more. We engage richly in our family's needs regardless of how menial they may seem. We strive to fulfill our obligation as husbands, fathers, and sons to the best of our ability. We bring the same energy and enthusiasm to our relationships as we do to our profession, workout regiment or fantasy football team.

For many alpha men relational excellence at the office is counter-cultural. **If we make Jesus' example of ministering to others a priority, work environments will change forever.** And I believe bottom lines and investor returns would skyrocket.

God will teach us to love others unconditionally. We can lift colleagues up, understand and meet their needs, encourage, and compliment them. Trusting God also helps develop compassion for those who suffer—including the sick, friendless, and even the arrogant.

Consider a former tyrant boss. Why was he so bitter? Did he feel empty at work? Abandoned by others he counted on? Was he fear for his job security? Did he struggle at home with his wife or kids? Was he trapped by an addiction he couldn't defeat on his own?

While these questions may seem out of line, under the New Man Code they are appropriate. Bosses need a safe place free from condemnation and ridicule like everyone else—a secure environment that we can provide. Relational excellence means we build our boss up rather than trash him to our peers. We can reach out to our boss with a simple question or two.

I was scared stiff to cross the line of faith and work.

I had a client in my consulting practice that hired me full-time to run his sales team. At the time, he was my gravy train, my sole source of income. He traveled from the West Coast to New York every week to serve as CEO of a failing internet company. The tension at the firm and the cross-country commute was murder on his marriage and his family life.

One night, he and I stayed late to review paperwork for a series of layoffs. He was dreading the process of letting his people go. I had been in the same situation and understood how he felt. No amount of experience makes it easier to cut someone loose. He looked beat.

Suddenly, a thought came to my mind: *Pray for him.*

We had never discussed faith. Openly sharing spiritual perspectives in a client/vendor relationship was out of bounds! *Pray for him.* It seemed too risky and against my better judgment. Reluctantly, I decided to trust God's lead.

"Would it be alright," I asked tenuously, "If I prayed for you and your family tonight?"

My client nodded. He made no further comment. The room fell silent. *I blew it!* All night I tossed and turned worrying about what he was thinking. *Aaarrrghhh, I'm such an idiot!*

When I arrived the following morning, he called me into his office.

"Can you shut the door, please?" *Oh no!*

"I've been thinking about what you said last night," he continued, "in fact, I have been thinking about it all night." *I'm going to get canned!* Taking a deep breath he smiled and said,

"Dave, that was the kindest, nicest thing anyone has ever done for me." *Wow!*

Our relationship changed that morning. We were no longer client and consultant; we were two men looking out for one another. Over the years, our friendship continued. We discussed issues of leadership, character, faith and family. Both of us benefited.

Not everyone would react the way my client did. I've endured my share of retorts to a kind word offered in good faith. However, negative responses don't shake my trust in God.

Being scared to integrate faith at work is natural; relying on God is not. Remember, God is our protector and our provider. Trust Him. If we look to Him for help with any relationship, He will oblige.

## Personal Equity

My friend Bruce is one of the most influential men I've met. He has become a great mentor to me and is the man I seek first when tackling life's toughest challenges.

I didn't like Bruce initially. He was a quirky guy who ate rice cakes and quoted ancient luminaries. When he spoke, he flailed his hands in wild gesticulations. He'd ask, "How's your heart beat, bro?" Worst of all, Bruce had this annoying habit of standing too close to people.

I was uncomfortable around Bruce, and yet at the same time relaxed. He was too intrusive when we talked, but I became increasingly transparent. Though I never took to rice cakes, I eventually took to him.

Bruce had a unique aura. People connected with him in a way I had never witnessed. He couldn't advance their career, get them courtside seats, or hook them up with girls, yet bankers, entrepreneurs, salesman, actors, and musicians showed up week after week to be part of discussions he led. These successful alpha men each characterized Bruce as someone who impacted their lives.

I am an accomplished leader, but no teammate, frat brother, or staff member demonstrated such loyalty to me.

What made Bruce such an influential leader?

Bruce is in the personal equity business. He is an *investor* in people rather than a *consumer*. The capital Bruce endows to others is time listening, encouraging, exhorting, and coaching. Bruce entangles himself in men's lives to help us untangle. He has no hidden agenda (I looked) and is only interested in the development of others.

Bruce is a true friend. He is courageous enough to tell me the truth, not just what I want to hear. During my darkest days, Bruce helped me escape a downward vortex by shining light into the blackness of my soul. He tore down the walls around my heart, enabling the Spirit of God to emerge.

Because Bruce invested in me, I invest in others—not out of obligation or duty but out of gratitude. If a man with a wife and three kids spent hours up to his elbows in my crap, the least I could do was give my time to others. This is the multiplicative power of personal equity. **My life changed because another guy cared enough about me to invest his time.** Now, I invest in others.

Jesus perfected the practice of personal equity. He spent time teaching a group of average guys. Together this crew of uneducated fishermen, laborers, and lowlifes changed the world. They followed Jesus' example and invested in others, building multiple generations of men following Jesus' example.

If you get into the personal equity business, you too can be part of God's vision for transformation. The only capital required is time and courage. Each of us can practice relational excellence. All of us can be men of integrity.

Jesus set this example, and others follow. This is the power of the New Man Code. The multiplicative effect can change your workplace, your community, and your city.

**You can be the catalyst for a movement.** It can start as soon as you invest in another man.

# TWELVE

# Leave No Man Behind

## A New Brotherhood

The battle of Alpha Man vs. God is for command and authority. Our fallen nature puts Self in control. Our instincts protect the position of Self on the throne of our life even if it means isolating ourselves.

Men need relationships with God and one another. Jesus tells us "Love the Lord with all your heart, soul, and mind,"[49] and "do unto others as you would have done unto you."[50] **The significance we seek can only be fulfilled by a relationship with God.**

Living a New Man Code is not a one-man show. Loving God with our hearts, souls, and minds is a tall order. We need other men to help us. In fact, asking for help is as important as giving it—both actions develop our relationships with one another and with God.

**Leave No Man Behind is a call for solidarity among the brotherhood of men.** We commit to help one another live well and willingly sacrifice on behalf of others. A military squad would never leave one of it's wounded behind. With the New Man Code, a platoon of men looks out for each other.

The film *Saving Private Ryan*[51] depicts such camaraderie. Captain Miller (Tom Hanks) leads a squad behind enemy lines to find Ryan (Matt Damon), whose three brothers were killed in action, and return him home. In a climactic scene Miller locates Ryan defending a small bridge with the handful of men remaining from his troop. Miller orders Ryan to leave his post and return home.

"Why do I get to go?" asks Ryan. Pointing at the others, he continues, "They fought just as hard as me."

Miller is flummoxed by Ryan's response. He barks at the Private about disobeying orders and cites men killed trying to find him. Neither admonishment alters Ryan's attitude. Then, Miller tries a different tactic. "What do I tell your mother," he asks, "who has already lost three sons?"

Ryan rubs his chin and looks into the beleaguered faces of his crew, men he hardly knew only a short time ago. "Tell her I am standing with the only brothers I have left."

*That* is loyalty. *That* is brotherhood. *There* is a level of allegiance that bonds men together. Granted, it's Hollywood's version of a WWII foxhole, but it demonstrates what men yearn for—a powerful fraternity with one another.

In our youth, disclosure was a means of building deep friendships. We cracked jokes with our buddies, acted goofy, and opened up to get to know one another. **We all wanted to be known and to belong.**

The Alpha Man Code makes real friendships nearly impossible. We are directed to be an "army of one" rather than a band of brothers. Authentic discussions about internal conflicts and the burdens we carry are off-limits—so are transparency and vulnerability. We hang out and shoot the breeze but never delve into issues below the surface.

The New Man Code breaks these barriers and enables men to establish strong bonds with others. Men *want* these types of friendships. We *need* them because they provide:

- validation of our experiences,
- wise counsel and advice,
- examples to follow,
- encouragement and exhortation, and
- companionship (not feeling alone).

Leave No Man Behind means we are all on the same team. Men are no longer alone. Individualism and self-reliance are history. We'll learn from each other as we journey through life together.

Living a New Man Code, black or white, short or tall, boxers or briefs—nothing divides us. We're on call for one another just as God is on call for us. If a friend struggles we don't look the other way or complain it's not our problem. We extend a hand to help our brother because we know others will do the same for us.

## Any Guy's Garage

You may assume men aren't clamoring for a new brotherhood. Nobody bugs you for a deeper level of friendship. However, **guys scream for help at a frequency nobody else can hear.**

Men hurt all around us. These are our best friends, buddies from school, work colleagues, neighbors, even brothers and dads They bleed internally from the blows of emptiness and fear. While people surround them, they may still feel alone.

"I had no idea," we comment after their lives become a train wreck. "He never mentioned anything," we say as they are hauled off to rehab or jail.

Wake up guys! We may be the only friend willing to reach out to them.

## One Man's Story

*Two buddies were having brunch at a popular West Side restaurant. They were both in the real estate business, divorced, and disconnected from their children. Andy had an eleven-year-old daughter he had not seen in months.*

115

Jerry had a toddler born out of wedlock.

They discussed how to become better fathers and more active in their children's lives. Jerry cited biblical passages on parenthood and the role of God in one's family. While they worked out the implications of what they read, Andy shared his frustrations with his ex-wife as well as disappointment with his own behavior.

"Let me pray for you," Jerry said, and clapped a hand on Andy's shoulder. Andy felt uncomfortable about this gesture in public. Peeking out of one eye as Jerry prayed, Andy noticed two young businessmen next to them (less then two feet away in a crowded New York restaurant). These men stopped their conversation to listen.

When the prayer was over, the omelets arrived.

Salting his eggs, Jerry turned to the guys at the next table and asked, "Are either of you two fathers?" One of the men overlooked the intrusion and nodded. "My friend Andy and I were discussing the rigors of fatherhood," Jerry continued, "and how we could be better dads." The two men leaned forward in their chairs.

Jerry reviewed his dialog with Andy. Eschewing the Alpha Man Code doctrine against vulnerability, he acknowledged his own failures and regrets for being selfish with his son. The two men were captivated.

"We are committed to re-establish relationships with our children," said Jerry, "and we hold each other accountable to God's will for us as fathers."

As Jerry spoke, one of the men grew emotional. "I just flew in from L.A. last night," he stammered. "I'm trying to reconnect with my daughter. We've been estranged for years." Tears streamed down his cheeks. "I don't know if she will even see me."

The four men pulled their tables together. Fatherhood was the topic of conversation. Together, they discussed how to rebuild trust with their families and God's role and pro-

*vision in these relationships.*

*As they rose from the table, a man from L.A. hugged a man from New York who he had known less than an hour. He was grateful for Jerry's transparency and candor. He appreciated the advice and encouragement. Even his close friends had not reached out to him in this way and he would not forget the kindness.*

*This man from L.A. now had hope. With that hope, life with his daughter would be different.*

---

Jerry and Andy were not schooled in counseling or anointed as clergy. They were just two guys like you and me. They were willing to ask an extra question. They were courageous enough to be authentic and share their struggles. The impact for themselves and others was dramatic.

You can be a spark for change, too. **Take it upon yourself to initiate a conversation with your friends or colleagues on subjects of substance.**

Here's a way to get started. Call up a handful of your buddies. Invite them to your place and head to the garage. Pull up some metal folding chairs and pour them coffee. Indulge in small talk, but then get down to business. Below are some questions to ask:

- If you were free to do anything, what would it be?
- In what area (beside work performance or time with the kids) would you like to experience significant personal growth?
- Are you nagged by a lack of meaning or fulfillment in your life?
- What's your biggest fear, one you feel you *can't* share even with your wife or family?
- Ever feel like you are all alone? As if you carry the burdens of life without any help?

117

- If you had five minutes with God, what would you ask Him? (Why He let that ball go under Buckner's glove in the '86 Series won't take the entire five minutes.)
- Do you know where you stand with God? Does that matter to you? Why or why not?

The mood may be uncomfortable at first. Guys will crack jokes, rib each other, and question your motives. They'll shift in their chairs, examining the ceiling or the tops of their shoes. Hang in there. Be patient.

These questions may seem intrusive. Some guys will feel you are getting too real. Talking about issues like purpose or meaning or God is awkward. That's the point.

Brew more coffee. Keep the conversation moving. Be the first to open up. Share your struggles and fears. Talk about the real issues on your heart. Someone else will follow. You'll see heads nodding in agreement. Ask more questions. The discussion will gain momentum.

At the end, set up a time and place to meet again. The discussion you initiate could be exactly what a friend needs but could never find. He will be sincerely grateful.

**Life change can start in any guy's garage.**


## Life: Raw and Uncut

Some of your friends may want a more challenging, in-depth experience. They need a safe place to talk authentically about what's hidden inside.

Several men's organizations hold stadium rallies challenging guys to reach new levels of honesty and self-examination. While attendees experience change during these events, the feeling rarely lasts beyond the confines of the gathering. Guys tell me that they lack context in their daily lives to integrate such levels of vulnerability, accountability, and encouragement.

Personal spiritual development falters without a safe venue to confront our toughest issues on a regular basis.

In New York, I am part of a more granular approach. Our grassroots effort to activate the New Man Code is to form DEEP Five groups. **DEEP Five groups are weekly, men-only gatherings of five guys asking each other five tough questions.** Together we examine life, raw and uncut.

The elements of DEEP Five gatherings are:

- **D**iscipleship
- **E**ncouragement
- **E**xhortation
- **P**rayer

DEEP Five provides a way for men to help each other tackle life's battles head on. In the security of these groups, we can build solidarity and assist one another to become the men God meant us to be. **God is part of a DEEP Five group.** Whether you know God or not, He'll be there.

In New York, men have taken to DEEP Five. Many *make* the time, rearranging their schedules to be part of these groups. After a month in his DEEP Five one friend called me and said, "These guys will *never* miss our group."

Five guys is a good size. With too many people, the intimacy of a group diminishes. With too few people, attendance can become a problem.

While not every guy makes it every week attendance has been remarkably consistent. Regardless of their vocation, marital status, age, ethnicity, or spiritual maturity men commit themselves to DEEP Five and to one another. And the development of their relationship with God has been off the charts.

If you are willing to examine the depths of your soul and the reality of your character, to boldly go where you have never gone before, **DEEP Five groups provide the context and means to experience transformation.** You'll need courage to be honest and face your fears. These five-man huddles are opportunities to exercise personal equity, invest our time in other men, and build relational excellence.

The key to men's meaningful experience in DEEP Five is the rigor of the questions we ask. They cut to the meat of the matter. There is no wiggle room, and nowhere to hide.

We all know a workout won't make us stronger if we don't challenge our limits. The same is true for our character and spiritual life. We must ask provocative questions to stimulate our relationships with each other and God.

Below are some guidelines for DEEP Five questions:

1. How is your relationship with God?
    a. Do you read the Bible regularly?
    b. Do you pray daily?
    c. When challenged, do you turn to God (rather than Self)?
1. How is your sexual integrity?
    a. Are you faithful to your wife, physically and mentally? Does your sex life meet *her* needs?
    b. Are you forthright with your girlfriend about your feelings and intentions? Do you abstain from premarital sex?
    c. Do you struggle with pornography? How are you addressing this problem?
3. How is your workplace integrity?
    a. Do you face temptations to get ahead which could compromise your integrity (i.e., shading the truth, cutting corners etc.)?
    b. Are you fully truthful to co-workers, clients, and third parties?
    c. Do you keep your promises and commitments?
4. Are you the best steward of the financial resources God gives you? How do you allocate your time and money to serve Him?
5. Do you share God's story and His impact on your life with others?

Hopefully, when a guy in your DEEP Five faces hard times, he'll reach for the phone rather than a bottle, a fix, or seclusion. "Hey bud, can we grab coffee? Something's going on that I need to talk about."

When you witness a hopeless man filled with hope or a helpless man empowered, you will glimpse the redemption available to all of us. When one man's marriage rebounds or his career gets back on track or he defeats an addiction, you will know the value of DEEP Five. You will be part of God's family business, and it will feel natural.

The time you invest in other men *can* change the world.


## Final Thoughts

Thanks for letting me share my story. I truly appreciate your time. I hope you find the journeys of other alpha men and insights on the unwritten Alpha Man Code helpful and thought provoking. I tried to write perspectives on God and Jesus to dispel rumors and errant assumptions as well as demonstrate God's relevance to men today.

The purpose of this book is to spark conversation among men. Together, we can re-examine our principles, convictions, and core values. Making space and time to talk about conflicts in our lives as well as radical paradigms can strengthen our character and relationships.

I recognize the difficulty of change and ceding authority of our life from Self to God. This is not an easy decision, and requires time and careful consideration. Transformation is the first step. Following God's will for us daily is a bigger hurdle. Fortunately, God provides practical tools. The Bible contains a rich collection of case studies for men; it is a book of God's wisdom, songs, and prayers, as well as accounts of Jesus' life and teaching.

Biblical narratives of Moses, Jacob, Joseph, Saul, David, Nehemiah (the best leadership book anywhere), Solomon, Job,

Daniel, the apostles, and others teach us how to integrate God in our lives. These accounts are real-life experiences of success and failure we can apply to our lives.

The Book of Proverbs is a library of wise counsel for the challenges and conflicts we face regularly. The Book of Psalms is an emotionally potent source of hope and renewal. The gospels of Matthew, Mark, Luke, and John illuminate Jesus through His own words and reassure us of God's promises of love and redemption.

Jesus said, "I came that they may have life and have it abundantly."[52] Purpose, meaning, peace and joy are the fruits of an abundant life. A relationship with God is the source. Building this relationship is an adventure of new frontiers, learning, growth, risk, reward, and excitement for the future.

My life has been transformed through this bond. Other alpha men's lives have as well. I hope it's a path you will consider.

I wish we could grab a cup of Joe together so I could hear your story. I'm sure it is fascinating and full of opportunity.

Like you, I hope to make an impact. With God at our side, any of us can have a life of significance. I look forward to getting there together.

# Endnotes

## Chapter One

1. *Gengarry Glen Ross.* Dir. James Foley. Artisan Entertainment, 1992.
2. Haggai 1:6 (All Bible references: *New International Version Bible.* Colorado Springs, CO: International Bible Society, 2007.
3. Easterbrook, Gregg. "The Real Truth About Money." *Time Magazine* 17 January 2005: A33.

## Chapter Two

4. *Fight Club.* Dir. David Fincher. Twentieth Century-Fox Film Corporation, 1999.
5. Hemingway, Ernest. *A Moveable Feast.* New York, NY: Scribner, 1964.
6. *The Godfather.* Dir. Francis Ford Coppola. Paramount Pictures, 1972.

## Chapter Three

7. CBS Interactive Inc. Tom Brady on *60 Minutes*, June 2005. *http://www.cbsnews.com*
8. Ecclesiastes 2:10-11 (NIV)
9. Frankl, Victor. *The Unheard of Cry for Meaning.* New York, New York: Simon & Schuster, Inc., 1978.
10. Warren, Rick. *The Purpose Driven Life.* Grand Rapids, MI: Zondervan Publishing House, 2002.
11. King, Jr., Martin Luther. *Stride Toward Freedom: The Montgomery Story.* New York, NY: HarperCollins Publishers, 1958. Emphasis added.
12. Solzhenitsyn, Aleksandr. *The Gulag Archipelago.* New York, NY: HarperCollins Publishers, 1985. Emphasis added.

## Chapter Four

13. *Troy.* Dir. Wolfgang Peterson. Warner Brothers Pictures, 2004.
14. Lewis, C.S. *Mere Christianity.* New York, NY: HarperCollins Publishers, 1943.
15. Franken, Al. *I'm Good Enough, I'm Smart Enough and Doggone It, People Like Me.* New York, NY: Random House, 1985.
16. 1 Corinthians 4:4 (NIV)

## Chapter Five

17. Wooden, John and Steve Jamison. *Wooden on Leadership.* New York, NY: McGraw-Hill, 2005.
18. Bennis, Warren and Burt Nanus. *Leaders.* New York, NY: HarperCollins Publishers, 1985.
19. King, Jr., Martin Luther. *Stride Toward Freedom: The Montgomery Story.* New York, NY: HarperCollins Publishers, 1958.
20. Romans 5:3-5 (NIV)

## Chapter Six

21. Chris Burge, used with permission.
22. Frankl, Victor. *Man's Search for Meaning.* Boston, MA: Beacon Press, 1959.
23. Galatians 1:13 (NLT)
24. Acts 9:3-6 (NIV)

## Chapter Seven

25. *Jaws.* Dir. Stephen Speilberg. Universal Pictures, 1975.
26. Cloud, Henry. *Integrity: The Courage to Meet the Demands of Reality.* New York, NY: HarperCollins Publishers, 2006.
27. Ecclesiastes 3:11 (NIV)
28. Proverbs 4:23 (NIV)

## Chapter Eight

29.     King, Jr., Martin Luther. *Stride Toward Freedom: The Montgomery Story.* New York, NY: HarperCollins Publishers, 1958.
30.     Assayas, Michka. *Bono: In Conversation with Michka Assayas.* Riverhead Books, 2007. Emphasis added.
31.     John 3:16 (NIV)
32.     Galatians 4:7 (NIV)

## Chapter Nine

33.     Assayas, Michka. *Bono: In Conversation with Michka Assayas.* Riverhead Books, 2007. Emphasis added.
34.     *The Passion of the Christ.* Dir. Mel Gibson. Newmarket Films, 2004.
35.     ABCNews Internet Ventures 2008. Mel Gibson, interview with Diane Sawyer. http://abcnews.go.com
36.     Luke 11:39, 41 (NIV)
37.     Matthew 23:3-6 (NIV)
38.     Coleman, Robert. *The Master Plan for Evangelism.* Grand Rapids, MI: Flemming H. Revell, 1963.
39.     John 13

## Chapter Ten

40.     Galatians 4:6 (NIV)
41.     *Hoosiers.* Dir. David Anspaugh. Orion Pictures Corporation, 1986.

## Chapter Eleven

42.     Proverbs 19:21 (NIV)
43.     Bennis, Warren and Burt Nanus. *Leaders.* New York, NY: HarperCollins Publishers, 1985.
44.     Carter, Stephen. *Integrity.* New York, NY: Harper-Collins Publishers, 1996.
45.     Luke 12:2, 3 (NIV)
46.     John 8:32 (NIV)

47.    Mark McCloskey, used with permission.
48.    1 John 4:19 (NIV)

## Chapter Twelve

49.    Luke 10:27 (NIV)
50.    Matthew 7:12 (NIV)
51.    *Saving Private Ryan.* Dir. Stephen Spielberg. Dream Works Distribution, 1998.
52.    John 10:10 (NASB) *Holy Bible, New American Stadard Version.* Nashville, TN: Holman Bible Publishers, 1981.

# Bible Quotations

## Chapter Six
Text from p. 63-64:
> "When traveling to Damascus, as Saul and his two colleagues were walking, he was struck down by a brilliant light.
>
> "'Saul, Saul why do you persecute me?'
>
> "'Who are you, Lord?' Saul asked.
>
> "'I am Jesus, whom you are persecuting,' He replied. 'Now get up and go into the city and you will be told what to do.'"

From Acts 9:3-6 (NIV):
> 3 As he neared Damascus on his journey, suddenly a light from heaven flashed around him. 4 He fell to the ground and heard a voice say to him, "Saul, Saul, why do you persecute me?"
>
> 5 "Who are you, Lord?" Saul asked.
>
> "I am Jesus, whom you are persecuting," He replied. 6 "Now get up and go into the city, and you will be told what you must do."

## Chapter Seven
Text from p. 72:
> "God has set eternity in the hearts of men."

From Ecclesiastes 3:11 (NIV):
> He has also set eternity in the hearts of men.

## Chapter Nine
Text from p. 92:
> "'You Pharisees are so careful to clean the outside of the cup and dish, but inside you are still filthy—

full of greed and wickedness!' He continued, 'So give to the needy what you greedily possess and you will be clean all over.'"

From Luke 11:39, 41 (NIV):

39 "Now then, you Pharisees clean the outside of the cup and dish, but inside you are full of greed and wickedness. 41 But give what is inside the dish to the poor, and everything will be clean for you."

Text from p. 92:

"'Do not follow [the Pharisees'] example. For they don't practice what they teach. They crush you with impossible religious demands and never lift a finger to help ease the burden.'"

From Matthew 23:3 (NIV):

3 "So you must obey them and do everything they tell you. But do not do what they do, for they do not practice what they preach. 4 They tie up heavy loads and put them on men's shoulders, but they themselves are not willing to lift a finger to move them.

Text from p. 92:

"Everything they do is for show...And how they love to sit at the head table at the banquets and in the most prominent seats in the synagogues! They enjoy the attention they get on the streets and they enjoy being called, 'Rabbi.'"

From Matthew 23:6, 7 (NIV):

6 "They love the place of honor at banquets and the most important seats in the synagogues; 7 they love to be greeted in the marketplaces and to have men call them 'Rabbi.'"

Text from p. 93:

> "Since I, the Lord and Teacher, have washed your feet, you ought to wash each other's feet. I have given you an example to follow. Do as I have done to you."

From John 13:14,15 (NIV):

> "Now that I, your Lord and Teacher, have washed your feet, you also should wash one another's feet. 5 I have set you an example that you should do as I have done for you."

## Chapter Twelve

Text from p. 113:

> Love the Lord with all your heart, soul, and mind.

From Luke 10:27 (NIV):

> You must love the LORD your God with all your heart, all your soul, all your strength, and all your mind.

Text from p. 113:

> ". . . do unto others as you would have done unto you."

From Matthew 7:12 (NIV):

> So in everything do to others what you would have them do to you, for this sums up the Law of the Prophets.

CPSIA information can be obtained at www.ICGtesting.com
Printed in the USA
BVOW082309280612

293838BV00006B/9/P

9 780615 157894